# THE ETATIST TURKISH REPUBLIC AND ITS POLITICAL AND SOCIO-ECONOMIC PERFORMANCE FROM 1980–1999

*A Developing State Impacted by International Organizations and Interdependence*

Dora Nadolski

University Press of America,® Inc.
Lanham · Boulder · New York · Toronto · Plymouth, UK

Copyright © 2008 by
University Press of America®, Inc.
4501 Forbes Boulevard
Suite 200
Lanham, Maryland 20706
UPA Acquisitions Department (301) 459-3366

Estover Road
Plymouth PL6 7PY
United Kingdom

Library of Congress Control Number: 2007940650
ISBN-13: 978-0-7618-3973-6 (paperback : alk. paper)
ISBN-10: 0-7618-3973-9 (paperback : alk. paper)

⊖™ The paper used in this publication meets the minimum
requirements of American National Standard for Information
Sciences—Permanence of Paper for Printed Library Materials,
ANSI Z39.48—1984

# Contents

# Preface

The author's principal message is to establish a discerning awareness for understanding the political, economic and social challenges Turkey has confronted in its quest for EU membership. This discernment for understanding began with Ataturk's mandated reforms, enabling Turkey's interaction with Europe. A trusted military hero and political leader, Ataturk's replacement of Islamic law with the Swiss Civil Code of Law has continued to assist Turkey with its ongoing efforts to comply with the EU *acquis communautaire,* a legal document for all prospective EU members. It is important to realize the distinction between internal reforms initiated by a nation's own leaders, as opposed to external reforms led by un-trusted leaders. External reformers usually experience warfare, whereas, internal reformers are dedicated to the interests of their nation and to its people. The reform process is continued by those Turkish leaders who have vowed to preserve the secular democratic republic established by Ataturk.

Those same leaders who have encountered reprisals, experienced coalition governments, recoiled and recovered from military coups, continue the quest to fulfill the label "the rest of Europe" attributed to Turkey by the World Development Report of 1997. Turkey's leaders of the secular republic have also experienced economic shifts, interrupting continual EU membership requirements. During the initial stages of membership preparation, the state-managed development model prevailed. Then the second shift ushered in neo-classical liberalized economic policies with conditional loans, granted on the basis that Turkey would begin to privatize state-managed enterprises. This shift required an incorporation of the state-managed plan with a liberalized market model. The third economic shift, a middle ground approach, was focused upon an appropriate division of labor between the state and the markets. The theory was based upon the idea that government intervention in the markets should determine which organizations would be privatized or unchanged.

A discerning awareness of Turkey's leadership during the past forty-three years of tumultuous economic shifts has demonstrated compliance with recommendations from the OECD, the World Bank and the EU in current efforts to fulfill the 2007 EU accession reviews. This discerning awareness of leadership will continue to be tested during the next seven years, as the secular establishment monitors President Abdullah Gul, elected on August 28th, 2007. President Gul, former foreign minister, represents the Justice and Development Party, with ties to a former Islamic affiliated party, a threat to the secular establishment. As foreign minister, Gul was instrumental in promoting the continuation of EU membership; now as president, he has pledged to sustain the separation of state and religion. During the Justice and Development Party tenure, under Prime Minister Recep Erdogan and now President Gul, Turkey's economy has grown seven percent each year, inflation has been abridged, and foreign investment has increased. EU Commission President, Jose M. Barroso, saluted Gul's election as advantageous to the accession process. Discernment, awareness and comprehension are essential to the perception of the obstacles Turkey continues to encounter as the democratic republic evolves.

# Tables

# Abbreviations

| | |
|------|-----------------------------------------------|
| ANAP | Motherland Party |
| BSEC | Black Sea Economic Cooperation |
| BOP | Balance of Payments |
| CAP | Common Agricultural Policy |
| CBRT | Central Bank of the Republic of Turkey |
| CHP | Republican People's Party |
| DSP | Democratic Left Party |
| DYP | True Path Party |
| EMU | Economic and Monetary Union |
| EPU | European Political Union |
| EU | European Union |
| FP | Virtue Party |
| GNA | Grand National Assembly/Parliament |
| HADEP | People's Democratic Party |
| ILO | International Labor Organization |
| IMP | International Monetary Fund |
| MHP | National Movement Party |
| NSC | National Security Council |
| OECD | Organization for Economic Cooperation and Development |
| PKK | Kurdish Workers Party |
| RP | Welfare Party |
| SEE | State Economic Enterprise |

# Chapter 1

# Perspectives and Introduction to Chapters

## The Theoretical Perspectives of Interdependence, Pluralism and Globalism

Products in international markets are subject to regulatory procedures, preference by purchasers, and intense competition facilitated by product specialization. Many developing states experience difficulty in gaining access to markets in more economically advanced countries. Therefore, the developing nations are intent upon gaining membership in regional trade organizations that will grant access to relatively tariff-free markets, as well as providing assistance in technological development, and, in some cases, a share in a common external trading bloc.

Entry into a regional trade organization may be a difficult and complicated process, especially if the composition of any one of these organizations is dominated by economically advanced states. The developed nations, through their influence in these organizations, have established regulatory procedures and rigid criteria for membership. This book is a case study of the reforms of Turkey's internal political and economic structures and policies as part of its quest for full membership in the European Union (EU). As a member of the Organization for Economic Cooperation and Development (OECD) since 1963, Turkey has profited from the recommendations, economic analyses and assistance provided by this organization. The political and economic reforms required from Turkey for full EU membership have been partially addressed, although remaining issues must be resolved.

Theoretical perspectives that provide an explanatory framework for the case study of Turkey's responses to external pressures are interdependence, pluralism and globalism. Interdependence is a situation of mutual reliance upon the products and services flowing between states. As such, it is proportional to state capabilities and levels of economic development. It is conditioned by the availability of resources, is asymmetrical, and may cause vulnerability for states struggling to adjust to, or to compensate for, external and internal pressures and changes (Keohane and Nye 1977, and Keohane 1990). The pluralist analysis is concerned with transnational interactions and relations among private and public individuals, groups and agencies inside individual states, below the top levels of government, and across state lines (Viotti and Kauppi 1993). Furthermore, both interdependence and pluralism occur in the global capitalist economy in which states are differentiated by developmental levels (see Appendix I).

In the international competitive markets, developing states need purchasing power for those products they do not produce. Moreover, technological advances facilitate further product specialization in states with the capacity to promote research and development. Therefore, developing nations with insufficient technology and limited market access, are compelled to join regional organizations that provide aid and assistance for technological development. Continual product specialization by each nation results in interdependence among nations because each national economy must rely on imported goods that it does not produce, or is unable to produce.

As indicated above, interdependence is a condition for interaction among states. Interdependent relations between the developing and developed nations may expose the former to particularly high levels of "sensitivity" and "vulnerability" as designated by Keohane and Nye (1977). These levels of sensitivity and vulnerability are the principal measurements of the asymmetry that often identifies economic relations between developing and developed states. Sensitivity to interdependent actions may be experienced by a developing state responding to the transaction costs involved in privatizing its state controlled economic enterprises (as recommended by the OECD); and vulnerability to interdependent decisions may result if those costs exceed the capacity of the government to respond to necessary political and economic adjustments that are involved in the privatization processes. Another dimension of interdependent sensitivity and vulnerability involves developing states engaged in world trade. For a developing state, the level of involvement in world trade directly affects its level of sensitivity and vulnerability to market fluctuations. Therefore, developing states, in their attempts to avoid varying degrees of sensitivity and vulnerability, seek membership in international organizations that provide preferential trading arrangements. These arrangements are regional, integrated, and eliminate restrictions on international trade and payments. If a developing state can meet the criteria for membership in the EU (a preferential trading arrangement), it may avoid varying degrees of sensitivity or vulnerability to market conditions by circumventing tariffs and adjustments to its balance of payments.

Asymmetrical interdependence has ties to conventional economic theory and relates to the interconnectedness of separate state economies and their levels of interdependence. "Demand interdependence" refers to the demand for each state's products from both national and international purchasers, and in the developed and developing nations. "Supply interdependence" refers to the dependence of developed nations upon the raw materials and products from the developing nations, and the dependence of developing nations upon the industrial products from the developed nations. Interdependence in both supply and demand is asymmetrical, and the economic disproportions between the developed and developing nations have been only partially alleviated by global Keynesianism. The strategy of global Keynesianism suggested that developed industrial nations and international organizations and institutions should transfer resources to the developing states for the purpose of initiating growth. The result should be mutual growth for both developed and developing nations (Martinussen 1997, 71-72).

Asymmetrical levels of economic interaction could result from a variety of factors; however, the capitalist world economic system is a principal facilitator of asymmetrical interdependence. The capitalist economic system remains dominant; the developing nations are scrambling to join world markets; and international institutions and organizations controlled by the developed states are pressing developing nations in their efforts to restructure internal economic, political and social policies. The restructuring of a state's internal policies can become an arena of conflict for those developing states reluctant to change or acquiesce to measures of control from external organizations or institutions:

Economic interdependence and its regulations have altered notions
of sovereignty: Few states can still demand to be completely independent of external authority over legal practices within their territories.
The best most states can hope for is to be able to use their sovereign
authority as a bargaining tool to assure that others also have to abide
by common rules and practices (Keohane 1998, 89).

International relations theorists distinguish between the theoretical
perspectives of globalism and pluralism with regard to the term "system." Pluralists address political processes, with a focus on the roles of
transnational organizations, bureaucracies, pressure groups, nonstate
actors, and interdependence in the international system. While the pluralists focus on parts of the political system, globalists emphasize the
consequences of economic hierarchy in the global system. Globalism
and pluralism do, however, agree that international issues are grounded
in political economy; that institutions, actors and organizations interact
within and between states and in the capitalist system; and that socio-
economic welfare issues are important at both the international and
national levels (Viotti and Kauppi 1993, 451). Interdependence within
the pluralist perspective is principally focused on international organizations, agents, actors and bureaucracies internal and external to
the state. Thus, pluralism is concerned with economic, political and
social issues resulting from differentiated interdependence among states
(Viotti and Kauppi 1993, 228-248).

The theoretical perspective of pluralism addresses the internal affairs of governments; considers that they may be impacted by external
organizations and institutions recommending changes; and that align-
ment of procedures and policies of developing states with those of developed international organizations may be in the interest of both. The shared
interests of developing and developed nations relate to market access for
their differentiated needs and to levels of interdependence resulting from
their interactions. The levels of economic and political interdependence
among the developing and developed nations are better understood through
the theoretical pluralist perspective, and the international capitalist markets are explained by both the globalist and pluralist perspectives.

The perspective of pluralism examines the state as a nonunitary actor; that is, decisions and policies within each state are the result of
competing individuals, interest groups, transnational organizations and
bureaucracies. Therefore, the strength and effectiveness of these poli-

cies and decisions assist in determining a state's capacity and its ability to interact with other nations. If civilian rule is interrupted by military intervention or coups, then a state's economic, political and social exchanges with other nations may be diminished or even terminated. Developing states experiencing such interventions have difficulties in meeting political and economic membership criteria established by international organizations aiding developing nations. Organizations such as the EU expect developing states to maintain a stable government consisting of democratic open elections, a multiparty system, a constitution, and a lack of military coups or interventions in governmental affairs. A stable democratic form of government is expected of states under consideration for EU membership. Expanding EU membership by accepting new states increases global integration of markets, and the principles of democratic government are augmented as states strive to democratize their internal structures. Therefore, developing states applying for EU membership into a system of democratic states are pressured to democratize their governments to conform to the system of government existing in the organization of EU states.

Levels of interdependence are affected by exogenous factors manifested in international organizations influencing and assisting developing nations. Although the level of interdependence among nations is also conditioned by endogenous factors affecting the ability or capacity of each state to formulate its internal policies, exogenous forces may assume a place of prominence when the government of a state is intent upon meeting an international organization's political and economic membership criteria for trade and other benefits. Developing states intent upon meeting criteria established by international organizations are aware that the changes required in their internal structures should assist in reducing the asymmetrical level of interdependence between developed and developing nations. In order to reduce this asymmetrical level of interdependence, developing states are currently encouraged by international organizations and institutions to focus on the competitiveness of their export products. As a developing state anticipates membership in and trade benefits from an international organization, internal governmental policies support plans for production of competitive exportable goods and services. Factors promoting competitive effectiveness include a stable government, domestic economic strength, infrastructures, and a general international perspective supported by the government and its

people. The need for developing states to produce competitive products to enter the markets within the system of interdependent states is
underlined not only by the OECD and the EU, but also by political
economists and rankings in the *World Competitiveness Reports and
Yearbooks* (Reich, 1990).

The research for this book principally relies upon the theoretical
perspectives of pluralism and interdependence. The capitalist world economic system (globalism) operates in a global context in which all states
and nations interact and function. Thus while nation states have differentiated internal plural political and socio-economic structures and institutions, they function and interact in the external global international capitalist system of interdependent states (Keohane 1990, Keohane and
Nye 1977, Martinussen 1997, Wallerstein 1980, and Chase-Dunn
1989).

## Application of the Theoretical Perspectives

The focus of this research is on the pluralistic interdependent status of
the developing state of Turkey as it interacts within the global capitalist
system comprised of other developing and developed nations and their
international institutions, organizations and separate governments. Nation states have differentiated internal units, and the external world system although consistently capitalist, is differentiated by unequal levels
of economic development and asymmetrical relations among states. States
with their institutions, organizations and actors/agents function internally and externally. If states exhibit similar political and economic patterns, as in "realism," then their differentiations do not appear to be a
theoretical or actualized problem. However, World Bank economic statistics and political stability studies indicate that nation states manifesting political differentiation are at varying levels of development as a
result of internal and external constraints and capabilities (World Bank
1997). Turkey with its governmental agents/actors and institutions,
functions at the national and global levels. Therefore the units for
analysis are dual.

Because capitalism is the principal global economic system, it facilitates interdependence among the separate states; international institutions
and organizations led by developed capitalist nations pressure developing states to change their internal political, economic and social structures to meet criteria for membership; and democratization of the politi-

cal system of developing nations may be a by-product of the processes. Turkey has been pressured to change its internal political, economic and social structures to comply with the criteria and recommendations from the international institutions and organizations, the OECD and the EU.

Although Turkey has been a member of the OECD since 1963, recommendations for internal change in its economic, political and social structures have been marked not only by the lengthy time-frame of privatization of their state-owned enterprises, but also by political instability (see chapter three). Moreover, Turkey's desire to join the EU has also been interrupted by its partial failure to meet full-membership criteria established by the EU Commission. This research will describe Turkey's legal, political and economic structures before 1980 and examine the transition of these structures from 1980-1999 in the context of influence by the OECD and Turkey's quest for membership in the EU.

Therefore, this study links Turkey to the interdependent world system of states, through the mechanisms of the OECD, EU and the World Bank.

In this research, economic interdependence in the global context is the independent variable. Turkey's interdependence with the EU and the OECD in world markets impacts the dependent variables: (1) democratization of Turkey's political and socio-economic institutions; (2) Turkey's membership in the OECD; and (3) candidacy membership status in the EU. The intervening variables periodically derailing Turkey from its intended objectives to westernize and Europeanize are: (1) the unresolved Kurdish problem; (2) accommodation of Islamic parties; (3) the threat of military intervention in the political processes; and (4) shifting economic policies at the international level.

As an observer during a three-year faculty residency in Turkey at Roberts College, Ankara Technical University and the Adapazari Lisesi, I obtained primary information from interviews conducted with political figures, judges, and military personnel concerning the political, economic and social structures of Turkey. These informal interviews support the argument for the secular republic and its membership in and affiliation with the OECD, the EU, and western alliances. These interviews are incomplete in that they do not reflect the views of the current Justice and Development Party (AKP), significant in the general election held on November 3, 2002. Data from annual OECD publications (1980-1999) have provided important information for analyzing the structuring and restructuring of Turkey's economic institutions and infrastructures. World Bank data were compared with OECD data to assess the problems a middle-income/developing nation faces when global economic policies and perspectives shift. World Bank criteria, developed for the purpose of measuring a state's capacity for effectiveness, were applied to Turkey's case.

## Chapter Previews

Chapter 2, a review of the literature, addresses the exogenous forces impacting Turkey's internal institutions and level of interdependence with developed states. Since the April 1999 elections, Turkey has addressed specific problems as a result of OECD and EU recommendations within a framework of interdependence. Primary and secondary literature sources discuss the political and legal legacy of Turkey. World Bank technical literature establishes criteria for state capabilities and effectiveness; OECD technical literature examines Turkey's progress from 1980-1999; technical and non-technical literature examines the criteria for Turkey's membership with the EU; and a variety of sources tap the supporting concepts of economic and political interdependence, pluralism, globalism, regionalism, and globalization.

Chapter 3 begins with a discussion of Turkey's Republic, the military tradition, its political interventionism, and its role as watch-dog protector of the secular republic. The chapter continues with a description of the restoration of civilian leadership, and public confidence in republican government after the 1980 coup. Military intervention might have occurred in 1997 had not the prime minister, leader of an Islamic party, resigned. Again an Islamic party won the November 3, 2002 general election. The AKP, with Islamic ties, had sufficient votes to form a new government without a coalition partner.

Chapter 4 discusses Turkey's capabilities as a relatively stable nation both politically and economically. It embraced the rule of law by adopting the Swiss Civil Code of Law in 1926. During 1980-1999, with assistance and recommendations from the OECD and the EU, Turkey achieved enhanced macroeconomic stability; improved the quality of social services; and protected vulnerable members of its society. Compliance with recommendations from the OECD, and access to the EU customs union have facilitated Turkey's entry into global markets, and informed it of product specification upgrades necessary for market competition.

Chapter 5 examines the annual OECD publications from 1980-1999 to determine the impact external organizations have had on privatizing Turkey's State Economic Enterprises (SEEs); improving the balance of payments; increasing the capacity of industry through product specialization; and assisting in infrastructure development. It describes the passage through parliament of economic restructuring legislation that had been approved and recommended by the OECD and the International Monetary Fund. The chapter continues with explanations for Turkey's changing policies resulting from three global shifts in western economic doctrines. Two economic shifts, Keynesian and neo-classical, created conflicts with Turkey's legacy of etatism (state-controlled enterprises). Then the third, a 1990s economic concept (supported by the World Bank), seemed to be a combination of liberalization and Keynesian government intervention. If industries and enterprises were profitable and well-regulated, then government should not intervene; however, if they were not, then government intervention was recommended.

Chapter 6 examines Turkey's candidacy status for EU membership. Prior to Turkey's acceptance as a candidate member in December of 1999, Prime Minister Ecevit succeeded in passing economic legislation considered as a significant step in Turkey's invitation to EU membership. This legislation (a partial continuation of the privatization of Turkey's SEEs and foreign investment regulations), had been regularly recommended by the OECD, but languished during Turkey's difficult political upheavals (the 1980 coups, weak coalitions and Islamic political party opposition). From the time former Prime Minister Bulent Ecevit skillfully engineered this recommended legislation through parliament, only four months elapsed before the EU announced Turkey's acceptance as a conditional candidate for membership.

Within the past two years, Turkey's political landscape has been changing as a result of dissatisfaction with the economy, Ecevit's failing health, and his inability to sustain voter confidence. These issues were factored into the recent general election by a majority of the voters casting their support for Recep Erdoğan, leader of the Justice and Development party (AKP), identified by its Islamic affiliations. After this recent victory, party leader Erdoğan, will undoubtedly spend his time influencing the current political establishment and the military that he is sincere about the acceleration of Turkey's full EU membership and integration into the global market economy. In the election of 2002, Erdoğan was selected as Prime Minister, and Abdullah Gül as Foreign Minister. Now in the current 2007 pending elections, with President Ahmet Sezer's seven year term near completion, Prime Minister Erdoğan presented Foreign Minister Gül as the AKP choice for president. This choice, discredited by the secular Turkish populace, led to mass public demonstrations in Istanbul, Ankara and other cities. Subsequently, the Constitutional Court declared the election illegal, and suggested Erdoğan select another candidate. As a result, an election may be rescheduled for June, July or November of 2007.

This chapter also discusses the EU in terms of regionalization and its role in eliminating the barriers to the flow of trade. Regionalization of states in the EU leads to product specialization for efficiency and control of those products produced by each state. This cyclical process results in the phenomenon of globalization, as more states become integrated into the EU, and as they begin to limit and specialize in specific products in competitive markets. Regionalization, globalization and specialization pressure nations to join economic organizations in order to compete in world markets. In order to compete, states must produce specialized products; and in order to produce competitive products, each state must reduce the variety of its goods and services. This cycle increases interdependence in the world system, but is also assists in strengthening Turkey's political and socio-economic institutions, and its relations with Europe and the rest of the West.

Chapter 7 concludes that Turkey experienced improved political and economic conditions from 1980-1999 in comparison with the difficulties encountered during the establishment of Atatürk's etatist republic. The new republic and its leadership chartered a course for a secular republic attempting to Europeanize its political, economic and social institutions. Before and during the secular republic, Turkey experienced and adjusted to the impact of exogenous forces and international organizations. OECD recommendations have changed Turkey's internal political and socio-economic policies, and the EU customs union has facilitated access to competitive international markets. EU criteria for full membership will continue to change the dynamics of Turkey's institutions. Research findings indicate that interdependence, pluralism and globalism assist in explaining Turkey's internal response to external impacts in its search for export markets in a specialized competitive capitalist international system. This chapter concludes that application of the theoretical perspectives of political and economic interdependence, pluralism and globalism to the case study of Turkey has significantly contributed to the field of international relations.

# Chapter 2

# Turkey's Interdependence: A Review of the Literature

## Rationale for Literature Selection

The method of expression concerning the various genres of literature is by summary design. Although sufficient literature exists with regard to Turkey's Republic, there are limited academic case studies about the effects of interdependence on Turkey as a developing state. With the exception of sources devoted to the Huntington thesis (that Turkey should be classified with Islamic societies), the corpus of literature for this book is concerned with the impact international organizations have exerted on Turkey. The literature also assists in an understanding of the problems and reasons why the developing state of Turkey, in search of export/import markets, finds it expedient to join relatively tariff-free international organizations. The researcher assumed that literature discussing the international relations perspectives of interdependence, pluralism and globalism would provide theoretical support as presented in Chapter 1.

The sources in Chapter 1 indicate that interdependence may be asymmetrical, and state interactions may produce levels of sensitivity or vulnerability (Keohane and Nye 1977, Keohane 1990, and Martinussen 1997). As a developing state, Turkey's interdependence with developed nations may be asymmetrical, and state interactions may produce levels of sensitivity or vulnerability necessitating internal adjustments. Literature sources advocating pluralism and internal adjustments in the decision making apparatus focus on parts of the political system, whereas globalism emphasizes a hierarchical economy within the global system. Pluralists and globalists focus on and are grounded in both national and international political economy. Literature on globalism provides a context in which interdependent states at various levels of development are competing in globalized capitalist markets. The capitalist mode of production promotes highly specialized competitive products which increases interdependence among states. In this context, developed states are the recipients of the process of capital accumulation—a process that dominates and shapes the development of the global economy (Viotti and Kauppi 1993, and Wallerstein 1980). Therefore, developing states are disadvantaged with respect to the benefits of capital accumulation for the purposes of investment in technology, and in the production of goods and services. As a result of this disadvantage, Turkey endeavors to join international organizations that provide market access and assistance with investments and other policies and procedures.

Literature for Chapter 3 was selected for the purpose of demonstrating that Turkey has a history of affiliation with Europe which resulted in changing and supplementing Islamic law to accommodate different levels of interactions with secular law. These accommodations prior to the 1923 reforms introduce the reader to Turkey's acquaintance with and acceptance of subsequent changes and recommendations by international organizations. World Bank literature for Chapter 4 was selected to indicate that Turkey, as a republic since 1923, and as a developing state, has demonstrated capabilities which qualify it as a state with the capacity to meet international measures and standards for building a democratic nation state. OECD annual publications and other economic literature for Chapter 5 were selected for the purpose of conveying the importance, acceptance and implementation of technical recommendations for the improvement of Turkey's economic and social institutions. EU literature for Chapter 6 was selected to familiarize the reader with the basic structures of the EU and to specifically indicate that Turkey as a current customs union member must meet certain conditions for full EU membership.

The EU and other international organizations have regularly questioned the disposition of democratization within Turkey's political institutions. Democratization of political institutions and leadership among nation states is highly differentiated and it is also contested. Moreover, the lack of economic equality in the world economy is also demonstrated by separate state GDP/GNP performance levels (World Bank 1997). Addressing this economic inequality has been an objective of international organizations attempting to assist developing states. An initiator of a globalized economic foundation, the EU began as a European regional organization dedicated to creating an institution to eliminate the causes of war. The EU has gradually contributed to the globalized economic processes by including not only the exclusive original developed nations, but also middle-income states.

OECD sources have analyzed economic improvements for the advancement of separate member nations (OECD 1980-1999). Established in 1961 for the purpose of cooperative economic advancement, this organization includes a variety of nations at different levels of economic development. Further, global economic inequality has decreased as the middle-income developing nations have advanced the cause of less-developed nations through the establishment of trade relations. Objectives of middle-income/developing nations interacting with the less-developed nations are, however, basically the same reasons developed nations secure primary, non-manufactured goods from the lower-income states.

# Political and Legal Legacy

Modifications in Turkey's Islamic legal codes preceded the secularization of its Muslim institutions. Prior to the 1923 secularization process, sources discuss the supplementation of and changes in Islamic law in the *mecelle* and *tanzimat* reforms (Englehardt 1914 and Kaynar1954). These reforms assisted in conditioning the Turkish mass populace to the necessity for accommodating Europeans in their midst by supplementing Islamic civil law. Interacting with the European community required a secular civil code compatible with European systems, and acceptable to the newly-secularized Turkish Republic with its parliamentary system of government. Finalizing the decision in 1926 brought about the adoption of the *Medeni Kanunu*, the Swiss Civil Code of law, capable of facilitating Turkish and European interaction (Akgun 1967).

Subsequent development entailed the upheavals and conflicts experienced by a forward-looking state with plans for secularizing its political and socio-economic institutions (Ahmad 1993, Berkes 1964, Karpat 1982, Lewis 1968 and Toprak 1981). The manifestations of these upheavals and conflicts were embodied in military interventions in the affairs of civilian government. Turkey has a legacy of military heroes who became political officials and were revered by the mass populace (Lewis 1968 and Hale 1994). Military intervention and coups in 1960, 1971 and 1980 discredited the civilian and democratized leadership of the Turkish

Republic (Hanioglu 1995 and Birand 1987). Although civilian and demo-cratically elected officials were discredited in each of these coups, the pre-existing political structure was able to form new political parties and coalitions, and stabilize government operations sufficient for military withdrawal. The military also maintained its dedicated legacy to uphold Atatürk's secular republic by denouncing Islamic political parties (Rahman 1982). These Islamic political parties have been intent on securing seats in parliament in order to revitalize Islam in Turkey's political and social institutions. Although Islamic parties have been prohibited by the consti-tution, Islamists continue to hold power in parliament (Tapper 1994).

Politicians have accommodated Islamic parties to assist in forming coalitions led by secular political parties, and military care-taker govern-ments tolerate Islamic parties not in control of a coalition government (Geyikdagi 1984). Both civilian government and military personnel rec-ognize that Islamic parties can contribute to stability when they are granted a government voice. The Islamic parties are also cognizant that any at-tempt on their part to gain control of parliament would endanger the stability of the Turkish Republic (Heper 1994). Endogenous forces work-ing to influence Turkey's political institutions are the military, secular political parties and Islamic parties. Exogenous forces influencing Turkey's government are comprised of two entirely opposite forces. On the one hand there are the Muslim Middle East Arab countries willing to contribute vast amounts of money and resources to propel an Islamic party to power. Conversely, the EU states are concerned with limiting Islamic access to power and discouraging intervention by the military. The 1997 resignation of Prime Minister Erbakan, a member of an Is-lamic party, was an indication of endangered government stability. Both Islamic and military forces realized that Prime Minister Erbakan, after only one year in office, had gone too far with his plans to establish a Muslim Middle East trading organization. His plan called for Turkey to discontinue its pursuit for membership in the EU, and to concentrate its efforts on a Middle East Muslim economic organization. The military, realizing the dangers Erbakan and his Islamic party posed to Turkey's secular government, threatened intervention (Ayata 1996). Erbakan, unlike former leaders threatened by the military, did not wait for an ultimatum. Rather than subject Turkey to yet another military interven-tion, Erbakan resigned; and Turkey seemingly has begun a period marked by concern for electing non-controversial, secular political parties to parliament (Sakallioglu 1996).

The November 3rd, 2002 general election resulted in a resounding victory for the AKP Islamic affiliated party led by Recep Erdoğan. Rather than the military demonstrating against the Islamic affiliated AKP, mass demonstrations by Turkey's secular citizenry against the selection of Foreign Minister Abdullah Gül for president, occurred in April and May of 2007. Despite the economic growth Turkey has achieved during the past five years, apparently Prime Minister Erdoğan has created mistrust among those supporting the secular Republic of Turkey, as set forth by the reforms of Atatürk. By selecting for parliamentary approval, AKP current Foreign Minister Abdullah Gül as president, Erdoğan has indicated his continuing support for the Islamic affiliated AKP, and thereby inciting demonstrations against his choice.

# State Capability

Studies concerning state capabilities and a state's capacity to exercise and administer effective government have been compiled by the World Bank researchers concerned that states not in the core group of nations lacked the capacity to assimilate or adapt to changes produced by economic shifts. These economic shifts, Keynesian, neo-classical and liberalized Keynesianism, required a stable government with solid, yet flexible infrastructures to determine the mechanisms and degrees for necessary adjustments and changes. Neo-classical, liberalized economic policies were affirmed to thrive if government interventions were reduced. However, the question arose concerning the political and economic policies that should be pursued when certain markets were productive and others were unproductive. The argument was that productive markets should continue without government regulation or intervention; while unproductive markets should be examined and regulated until they could be targeted for privatization.

Apparently the World Bank decided that the 1997 world-scale project should focus on state capabilities. Although the World Bank study did not focus specifically on Turkey, the criteria established for state capability were applied to Turkey. OECD and International Monetary Fund recommendations, combined with World Bank criteria for effective administration of government, have been applied. Applying the criteria (rule of law, macroeconomic stability, social services/infrastructures, and protection of vulnerable societal members) to Turkey's state capabilities revealed that Turkey has implemented a secular political legal system, OECD economic policies, and a social security program. The aforementioned issue of vulnerable societal members, the Kurds in Turkey, reveals a human rights problem that must be addressed prior to granting full EU membership.

The issue of twenty million Kurds unassimilated into the mainstream of Turkey's political, economic and social institutions must be addressed according to the EU human rights charter and the Turkish constitution (see Appendices II; VI). Literature discussing the Kurdish problem cites Saddam Husayn's manipulation of the Kurdish Workers Party (PKK) during the Gulf War, the Abdullah Ocalan affair, and skirmishes on the contiguous Iraq, Iran and Turkish borders (Gunter 1992). Other than granting concessions for the use of the Kurdish language in conversation, restrictions by the Turkish government on the Kurds and their activities remain in force. The EU commission has informed Turkey that resolutions to the Kurdish issues must be in progress before full membership can be achieved. One impediment to possible solutions must be initially addressed to the satisfaction of the EU commission. Ocalan, leader of the Kurdish Workers Party, cannot be executed by government fiat. Turkey maintains that Ocalan has violated the constitution by attempts to establish a separate state for Kurds within Turkey, and he remains imprisoned. This researcher suggests a recommendation for proportional representation in Turkey's parliament for twenty million Kurds clustered in eastern Turkey. If thirty-two percent of Turkey's Kurdish population could become represented in parliament, perhaps issues could become legally and peacefully addressed. This proposal would also include methods for assimilation of the Kurdish population into the mainstream of the social, political and economic institutions of Turkey.

# The Organization for Economic Cooperation and Development

The 1980-1999 annual OECD technical publications have provided concrete data for analyzing the thesis that Turkey occupies the position as a state progressing from a lower to a middle-income/developing nation. While each publication provided data regarding the yearly status of Turkey's economy and recommendations for improvement, the 1999 publication was also important for summarizing actions for social legislation and the continuation of the privatization of its SEEs. This publication, unlike the regular recommendations, focused on social security (OECD 1999). As a result, parliamentary legislation was passed to alleviate the budget deficit imposed by early retirement.

Additional series of technical and non-technical publications have contributed to understanding prevailing economic policies as reasons for Turkey's reluctance to implement OECD recommendations from 1980-1998 (Carbaugh 1995, Martinussen 1997, Thomas 1991, and World Bank 1997). From 1980-1999 Turkey's economy was affected by global economic policy shifts. These economic policy shifts influencing the global economy were Keynesian purchasing power changes in surplus and deficit nations which could automatically help to restore payments to equilibrium when surplus nations experience increased imports and deficit nations face declining imports (Carbaugh 1995, 384). Two other shifts were the neo-classical liberalized trade policies for the 1980s-90s, and the World Bank middle-ground policy advocating state structure capacity-building with case by case government intervention for the 1990s. Turkey accommodated these three global shifts; and it factored in external OECD and World Bank recommendations that had been accepted by previous administrations, but became bills which were finally passed by parliament and approved by the president in 1999.

# The European Union

Sources discussing the foundation of the EU and its institutional components refer to the original community as an economic response to a political problem (Swann 1995 and Pinder 1991). The political problems continue as Turkey, an OECD member, attempts to meet EU political and economic membership criteria. The OECD has assisted Turkey in meeting economic criteria; however, political problems, both internal and external continue to prevent full membership. The Turkish/EU candidacy watch by those concerned with the veto power formerly exercised by Greece were not surprised to learn that EU membership candidacy was conditional. The EU commission stipulated that Turkey and Greece must settle all differences related to northern Cyprus. These settlements must be promoted through the International Court of Justice and reviewed by the EU Commission. Thus it is not entirely inaccurate for the EU/Turkish watch group to assume Greece lifted the veto on the condition that the EU commission would request settlement of the Cyprus issue (Ayata 1996 and Kadioglu 1996).

European and Turkish cultural differences have been voiced by the Turkish watch group since 1963 when Turkey first applied for EU membership. Regarding cultural differences, Huntington arbitrarily determines that Turkey would be a "torn state" if it continues the quest for European identity; that Turkey, in the classification of world civilizations could become a "core state" in the Muslim world (Huntington 1996). Supporters of the Huntington thesis, that Turkey is Muslim and is central to the Middle East bloc, ignore Turkey's quest for European identity. While the Huntington group denies Turkey's European identity, the same rationale (Turkey is Muslim) is used by some advocates for EU membership. This latter group, consisting of Turkish government officials, some business firm executives and authors maintain that Turkey was principally barred from EU membership because of its Islamic heritage; that the cultural differences between the EU core nations and Turkey's sixty-five million people were too diverse (that silence on this issue spoke against Turkey's capacity for European identity).

The literature also focuses on advocates concerned with strategic military reasons for consolidating Turkey's relationship with Europe (Pinder 1991). This position has merit based on recent reports that the EU has decided to create a rapid reaction force of fifty to sixty thousand soldiers by the year 2003. These forces would be deployed to crisis areas where NATO forces are not committed. Turkey has partially fulfilled political and economic criteria established for EU membership; however, some conditions must be addressed by the year 2004, and other conditions may require a flexible time-frame.

The cardinal literature under examination for this book focuses on the dynamics of causal factors that have promoted, and are promoting the prospects for the transformation of Turkey from a less asymmetrical level to a more symmetrical level of interdependence with the developed nations. The ensuing chapters are designed to indicate the importance of those exogenous causal factors impacting the endogenous internal political and socio-economic institutions of Turkey. The sources assisted in sequencing the chapters according to not only the chronology of causal factors impacting Turkey's internal institutions, but also the importance of, and the capacity of the state to act on these international recommendations. As a result, Chapter 3 presents historical information which conditioned Turkey to external influences. Chapter 4 demonstrates that Turkey's state capabilities are currently sufficient to meet criteria recommended by the OECD as presented in Chapter 5, and that these partially implemented recommendations have assisted Turkey in its conditional acceptance into EU membership as discussed in Chapter 6.

# The Rationale for Unit Analysis

The three *isms* as discussed by Paul Viotti and Mark Kauppi—globalism, pluralism and realism—offer three perspectives for understanding the interactions of nation states.

Globalism, as defined by Viotti and Kauppi focuses on capitalistic relations of dominance in understanding world politics. Pluralism assumes that non-state actors are important; that the state is comprised of interacting bureaucracies, groups and actors. Realism focuses on the power of the state as a unitary actor, its interactions with other states, and security issues. Interdependence is interaction between two or more states in which one is sensitive or vulnerable to the decisions or actions of others. Interdependence may be symmetrical; however it is usually asymmetrical. Complex interdependence (Keohane and Nye) refers to the multiple transactional channels connecting nation states with emphasis on economic interaction (Viotti and Kauppi 1993, 577-591). This research principally applies the international relations theoretical perspectives, globalism, pluralism, and interdependence to the case study of Turkey. The rationale for this decision is predicated on the assumption that since 1980, Turkey has been involved in political, economic and social concerns principally addressed by globalism and pluralism. Further, it appears that Turkey's well-established, powerful military (over six-hundred thousand), has been sufficient in safeguarding the nation as well as its contributions to the NATO forces. Thus, realism as a military perspective seemingly has not been at the forefront in identifying issues of the past two decades. The US led invasion in Iraq, and the continuing warfare, have involved Turkey's military at its border with Iraq. In May of 2007, additional tanks were sent to the border of northern Iraq where Kurdish guerrillas continue their exploits for self-determination in southeast Turkey. Despite the imprisonment of their leader, Abdullah Ocalan, the campaign for a separate Kurdish state continues.

Turkey, in its continual efforts to identify itself with Europe and the west, has succeeded in terms of the World Bank publications. For the past decade, these publications have classified Turkey as the "other Europe" rather than part of the Middle East. Turkey's strategic, geographical location situates it in either the Middle East or Europe. In October of 1999, Turkey forged an alliance with Israel—reported to include arms deals. By giving utmost importance to increasing defense cooperation, former Prime Minister Bulent Ecevit anticipated upgrading the fighter jets. Former Israeli Prime Minister Ehud Barak anticipated the sale of arms, joint naval maneuvers in the Mediterranean and cooperative, regional water projects. Both leaders assumed jointly funded projects for research and development in science and technology.

This alliance has already angered Syria as well as Saudi Arabia, involved in monetary support for any Islamic political party attempting to gain strength in Turkish politics. Turkey has been ridiculed by the European community for its treatment of Kurds who inhabit the contiguous borders with Syria, Iran and Iraq. Arab leaders, particularly Iraqi leader Saddam Husayn, have exploited the Kurdish Workers Party for their own purposes by supposedly supporting the Party's agenda. It may be too early to assume that Turkey has made a significant step in what appears to be further distancing from its former Middle East Islamic identity. It appears that Turkey is seeking to focus its Middle Eastern identity on relations with Israel, the only other western-oriented state in the general area with which Turkey has friendly ties. Referring to this alliance is important for future security issues. However, this book focuses on the Turkish political and economic problems identified within globalism, pluralism and interdependence.

The world system of nations from political and economic perspectives is comprised of the developed nations, the developing nations and the less developed nations. These terms can become operationalized when a nation state is identified (Turkey in the middle-income group of developing nations) and as it interacts (from a pluralism perspective) in the interdependent world system of nations. Turkey, a middle-income nation, is operative in the system of nations at the national and international levels through its interaction in the world system and its membership in the OECD, the World Trade Organization (WTO), the United Nations (UN), the EU customs union and various alliances with other nations. The distinguishing characteristics of the developing status of Turkey as opposed to the less developed nations are: Turkey is interdependent rather than dependent; Turkey is a member of the above-listed organizations; and Turkey has westernized and secularized its government and legal structures, thereby facilitating interactions with the western and European world. Focusing on Turkey as a case study (according to Lijphart) within the theoretical framework of globalism (Turkey, a world system middle-income nation) and pluralism (interdependence and complex interdependence), provides a context for examining causal and dependent variables applicable to other nation states.

Some theorists of international relations are in disagreement regarding the unit of analysis. Is the unit for analysis the differentiated, unequally developed nation states (developed, developing and less developed) competing in the world system; or is the unit for analysis the entire system of nation states viewed as like units competing for an increased share in the nation state system? The arguments defining international relations theory are not simplified by assuming that an issue or problem can be examined within the context of only one or the other units for analysis. Rather the arguments have expanded as problems and issues have arisen and are in need of evaluation. Although the national level of analysis assists international relations in examining differentiation within separate states, issues, problems or conflicts (if thoroughly understood in terms of their international context) also require a systems level approach. The unit of analysis defining states comprised of their societies, communities, interest groups, and bureaucracies (with political social and economic actors), are contrasted, compared or combined with the systems level, defined as the distribution of capabilities or power among states.

Moreover, the theoretical international relations arguments are not reducible to mere lexicon distinctions or preferences for classificatory terminology. Nor are these arguments engaged in redefining similar yet differentiated divisions of states within the system of nations. The researcher examining developmental literature notes that the terminology used to differentiate economic levels are developing, underdeveloped or developed; modern, pre-modern or post modern; and core, semiperiphery or periphery. Theorists insistent upon refining these classificatory divisions of nation states determine that the developmentalists are concerned with economic and political issues, whereas the modernization literature seemingly reflects the human reaction to levels of industrialized development.

The lexicon issue as it extends to the perspectives of the *isms* provides the macro and micro units of analysis for the purpose of rationalizing Turkey's interaction in the world system of nations. The globalist position is responsive to the systems level of analysis by examining the world capitalistic economic structure comprised of the differentiated developmental levels of separate states within the developed, developing, and the less developed nation states. The pluralist position is concerned with the agents/actors as the principal unit of analysis within each state (Turkey's key political actors and international economic agents). For research clarity, the unit of analysis is qualitatively and quantitatively important; however, from an ontological perspective and the necessity of international relations theory building, both national and international are the *modus operandi* of the world system. For example, pluralism as a national level of analysis cannot adequately analyze interdependence without examining how agents or actors interact with other nations in the global, world system. Turkey, a middle-income nation, interacts with the developed and developing states of the capitalist world system for both economic and political purposes. Disproportionate focus on either unit of analysis, exclusive of the other, disrupts the rationale for contextualizing issues within the international system of states. Moreover, ontology assumes the incorporation of both the national and international levels interacting in the world system rather than the disaggregation of states from actors whom they represent.

Thus the international relations issues are not defined by whether globalism, realism or pluralism separately addresses problems related to the unit for analysis debate. Nor are the problems a lexicon issue engaged in terminological distinctions. Rather, the important issues are concerned with structural differentiation in and among the units, the separate states at the national level as they function within the international system. Empirically and ontologically, the separate nations are structurally differentiated by not only their political and social systems, but their economical levels of development. These differences among states are explained by various theories; however, the emphasis of this research focuses on pluralistic interdependence within the context of nation states interacting within globalism. The parameters of this book define structures as the separate, differentiated nation state structures interacting within the world system structure. The logic is: nation states have differentiated, internal structures, and the external system is differentiated by the developed, developing and less developed states.

States with their institutions and actors function internally and externally. If states exhibit similar political and economic patterns, then their differentiation does not appear to be a theoretical or actualized problem. However, World Bank economic statistics and political stability studies indicate that nation states manifesting political differentiation, are at varying levels of development resulting from internal and external constraints and capabilities. For the purposes of research, the state of Turkey, its actors and institutions function at two levels of analysis: the internal state level and the external international level. Therefore the units for analysis are dual (in that Turkey represents a state unit functioning as a developing nation) within the international system of states.

# Chapter 3

# Atatürk's Reforms and the Turkish Republic

Interruptions in the flow of the Turkish political system have assisted as well as hindered the process of transformation. A review of Atatürk's reforms, etatism (state control of the economy) and secularism prior to 1980 is necessary for understanding the legacy of the 1980s and 1990s. The term republic (*aljumhuriyah*) was a familiar term to Muslims; however, a secular state, as planned and established by Atatürk, was unfamiliar to Islamic Turkey. The secularization process from an Islamic state to a republic was the difficult aspect of reform and transformation for the non-western, less-educated populace. Reform measures separating the state from Muslim law, and from a complete way of life established in the community of believers (*umma*), were equally difficult for the whole of society—although less problematic for those dedicated to turning to the West. Atatürk, a military hero respected and eulogized by an undivided Turkish community, initiated his reforms after negotiation and ratification of the Lausanne Treaty, the most important document internationally recognizing the legitimacy and independence of the emerging Turkish nation.

The Lausanne Treaty was signed on July 24, 1923 after Atatürk and his military forces had successfully waged a "war of liberation" against the Allies who were attempting to annex wealthy provinces from the defeated Ottoman Empire. These attempts to gain control of the spoils and territory of the former Ottoman Empire were drawn up under the terms of the Treaty of Sevres of 1920. However, the terms of this treaty were never enforced after Atatürk's military victories against the Allies. As a result of these military victories, the Allies had constructed the Treaty of Lausanne which replaced the Treaty of Sevres. After acceptance of the Lausanne Treaty, the Grand National Assembly (parliament) selected Atatürk as president of the republic. The Lausanne Treaty established Turkey as a sovereign nation, enabled Atatürk to begin reform measures, and abolished the special privileges granted during the Ottoman period to non-Muslims. These special privileges, referred to as capitulations, were numerous and especially resented by the Muslim populace. One segment of the Ottoman capitulations, economic concessions, established a pattern of reliance upon non-Muslim commercial agents who conducted daily business activities. They allowed a non-Muslim merchant class to purchase *berats,* certificates, from European embassies for the conduct of commercial privileges in the Ottoman Empire. The sale of these *berats* created a privileged class known as *Avrupa Tuccari,* or European merchants (Lewis 1968, 454-466).

Atatürk's military victories, the Lausanne Treaty, and the end of capitulations afforded an opportunity to introduce reforms to an emerging nation. In 1931 Atatürk published a manifesto of proposed reforms which were adopted by his Republican People's Party (*Cumhuriyet Halk Partisi)* in the same year. These reforms, known as "Kemalism" were: republicanism, nationalism, etatism (state control of the economy), secularism, populism and reformism. Atatürk intended to establish a secular, constitutional republic with sovereignty vested in a nation of Turks. The advocates of Kemalism envisioned a nation inspired to promote Turkish nationalism and populism (equality of the citizens of the republic); to support reformism (the legitimized method for implementing political, economic and social change); and to uphold the principles of the republic with its state separated from Islamic jurisprudence. To rid the nascent nation of economic foreign influence, Atatürk and his advisors determined that *devletcilik* (etatism), state economic control, would be an effective policy (Lewis 1968, 239-292). The Atatürk reforms, etatism and secularism in particular, significantly impacted Turkey's political, economic and social structures, and were therefore significant in the initial reforms.

Etatism did not deny private work and economic activity; however, the intent was to engage the emerging state in areas of vital national interest, and to direct the nation on a course of prosperity within a reasonable length of time. Atatürk declared that the economic policy of etatism "rests on the principle that the state must take charge of the national economy." (Lewis 1968, 287). Etatism was not an adaptation of socialism, nor a denial of private Turkish initiative; it was an attempt to address and mobilize the economic needs under a central authority for a new nation in need of direction and control. Private enterprise would retain a role; however, state government intervention would be necessary to bring about a level of prosperity based on five-year plans for creating public enterprises (later referred to as SEEs—state economic enterprises, and discussed in the Organization for Economic Cooperation and Development chapter). The Republican People's Party supported the concept that etatism was an intermediate position between capitalism and socialism; that it encouraged the tenets of private enterprise; and that it was a premise used to establish state controlled industries. Further, the party supported the idea that after Turkey reached an acceptable level of development, some state enterprises could revert to the private sector. During the etatist policy of the 1930s, Atatürk's government established import-substitution industries and a policy of protective tariffs (Kazancigil and Ozbudun 1981, 165-189). Etatism was and is an economic policy supported or repudiated by various political parties, and also conditioned by external recommendations as discussed in the OECD and European Union chapters. The rationale for Turkish etatism seemed to be linked with the idea that the state should be a provider of both political and economic endeavors in the attempts to stabilize and control a newly emerging nation.

Reform measures before Atatürk began in the Ottoman period during the *Tanzimat* Reform era from the latter half of the eighteenth century to1871.[1] At that time, the *Mecelle*, Islamic legal rules and some codified civil law,[2] was still an incomplete code, and unrecognized by foreign courts. The Ottoman Empire, a crumbling entity before it was reduced to Turkey's current geographic boundaries, struggled to meet the external, economic encroachments of the European Powers. At the same time, the empire endeavored to accommodate and adjust to these external pressures while confronting internal problems.

The question of civil law, an internal issue related to secularizing the political and legal structures, came to the attention of the Turkish nation after Atatürk succeeded in abolishing the Caliphate (former symbolic head of the Islamic world) in 1924. The abolition of the Caliphate effectively ended the link between the state and a Muslim nation; the *Şeriat*, the holy law of Islam, was revoked; *medreses* and *tekkes*, Islamic schools and Sufi convents were closed; plans for secular education were introduced; and capitulatory non-Muslim privileges were denied.

Western Powers, reluctant to accept Turkey's final push for total abrogation of the capitulations (as a provision of the Lausanne Treaty), served as justification for Turkey to examine the status of civil law (Lipstein 1957, 71). Atatürk, in favor of adopting a Western civil code, spent a two-year period from 1924-1926 persuading the nation and the Istanbul faculty of law of the importance of this examination of civil law (see note for an excerpt from Atatürk's speech).[3] Finally, after considerable deliberation and examination of various legal systems, the complete Swiss Civil Code, translated into Turkish, was accepted by the Grand National Assembly in 1926. This transaction meant the abandonment of the dual religious and secular court systems, final abrogation of the remaining vestiges of the capitulatory system, and the abolition of the *Mecelle.*[2]

The adoption of the *Medeni Kanunu*, the Swiss Civil Code, was a radical transformation in that it meant the disestablishment of family, marriage and inheritance law, the crux of Islamic law. The transformation carried with it the necessity of justifying its adoption:

> Modernization and secularization have been responsible for reception of foreign law in Turkey. . . . The adoption of the Swiss Civil Code was not such a revolutionary change, because it is the last stage in an evolution which had been going on beginning with the Kanun system. . . . Beneath the empire's religious super structure, a national and secular system of law was continually developing. . . . The revolution brought about by Atatürk did no more than put an end to the dualism of the earlier regimes. . . . Of course there were problems and clashes between the reformative spirit of the laws received and the conservative nature of the social set-up in the receiving country (Kubali 1957, 65-68).

Acceptance of a foreign law without an understanding or knowledge of how it would be interpreted or used could undoubtedly lead to some unfavorable results. First, interpretation of the new Swiss Code on the part of the legal authorities and scholars became an important issue. Since reasoning by analogy and interpretation was considered important to Islamic law, would it be utilized in the application of the Swiss Civil Code to Turkish cases? Would practices, customs and procedural methods from Koranic law apply to the newly adopted Swiss Civil Code? Turkish judges, whose style and training were different from that of *legistes* in Switzerland, were confronted with the tasks of the use of interpretation from Koranic law and its application to the new code. Therefore, after 1926, the faculties of law at Istanbul and Ankara universities trained judges and lawyers in the knowledge of Swiss civil law, the first step in implementing the new code.

Second, the legal structure was confronted with the problem of presenting the Swiss Civil Code to the masses primarily through the courts. Separate religious and secular court systems no longer existed. Disruption continued, however, since restructuring of the courts became necessary. All the lower courts had to adjust to trials involving family law and the difficulties of the new system. If the decisions from the lower courts seemed unsatisfactory, the case could be taken to the Court of Cassation, the highest court with no intermediate courts, where the case had to be reheard. In both situations, strict application of the code was to be the basis of decision making and not reliance upon whatever could be considered case law by precedence. This meant that the Court of Cassation was using the same methodology as the lower courts since it relied almost exclusively on the codes themselves. The marked difference, however, was the distinction in capability and understanding of the new codes on the part of the lawyers and judges of the Court of Cassation as opposed to those occupying the seat of judgment in the lower courts.

Third, the new Swiss Code had to be tested in response to family law. The villagers were consistently disobeying the new laws by marrying at whatever age they chose; moreover, they failed to register their marriages with the official *belidiye* (provincial, county office). Technically, the new law would not recognize these unregistered marriages and the children were considered illegitimate. If some remedy in the form of law had not been enacted regarding the question of illegitimacy, the legal system would have been confronted with even more difficult problems and conflicts respecting the matter of succession and inheritance. Who would inherit from the parents if their children were considered illegitimate? Regarding the possession of land, it was necessary to establish ownership through registration. This was somewhat revolutionary in that the villager became the rightful and legal owner of the plot of ground he had formerly cared for but which had been subject to the regulations of the state. This new system gave the villager freedom in that he could sell this land, keep the money and move to the city if he desired. Addressing these issues was accomplished by the Court of Cassation by actually writing law which changed the marriageable age, legitimized children of unrecognized marriages and made allowances for unregistered land. These decisions by the Court of Cassation would not necessarily be classified as having been derived from reasoning or interpretation, since one entailed a technical age change; the other decided to recognize the legitimacy of children born to parents who had not officially registered their marriage. The decision regarding land law, however, was based upon *sui generis* and therefore utilized interpretation and reasoning.

This discussion of the adoption of the Swiss Civil Code of law is important to understanding one of the most radical transformations Atatürk implemented in a former Islamic nation in its pursuit of the difficult task of becoming a republic. This concept of republic was compatible with Sunni Islamic theory of agreement (*bay'ah*) reached by consensus of those governed. Thus Atatürk met with limited opposition in his goals for the establishment of the Republic of Turkey (Velidedeoglu 1957, 51-85). Atatürk had established a secular republic; was successful in abolishing the vestiges of Islamic law and implementing the Swiss Civil Code; instituted the economic state control policy of etatism; and established a military legacy which has assumed the role of guardian of the secular status of the republic.

# The Turkish Republic and the Military Prior to 1980

The Turkish Republic's nascent beginnings were in the hands of the respected military leaders, Atatürk and İsmet İnönü. After Atatürk's death in 1938, İnönü was elected president and served as the chairman of Turkey's only party at that time, the Republican People's Party. By 1946, an opposition party had been created, the Democratic Party. This new party in the 1950 election ushered in Celal Bayar as the third president of the republic. After the election, he attempted to abandon etatism in favor of private enterprise by limiting the state's capacity to regulate the economy. As a result of this attempt to limit state regulation of the economic policy, excessive imported foreign goods and technology brought Turkey close to insolvency.

Adnan Menderes, appointed as prime minister in 1950, angered the intellectuals and the military with his corrupt policies. Menderes cultivated the support of the conservative Muslims intent upon restoring *ezan* (call to prayer), the *tarikats* (Sufi brotherhood orders) and *tekkes* (community centers and Sufi convents). These *tarikats* and *tekkes* had been abolished by the Atatürk reforms because they were in conflict with the objectives of the new republic. The *tarikats* and *tekkes* had been vested with a *sheyk*, or leader to whom members were committed. Moreover, the social fabric of society had been severed for those Muslims who were devoted to the Islamic concept of the community of believers (Mehmet 1990, 116-122). Restoration of Islamic institutions which had been abandoned by Atatürk's reforms were considered a threat to the secular republic by the military and some government officials. This level of dissatisfaction with attempts to restore Islamic institutions, and the serious economic problems during the Menderes and Bayar regime, set the stage for the military coup of May 1960.

This military coup led by General Cemal Gürsel resulted in the arrest of Menderes and Bayar who were found guilty of violating the Turkish constitution (Saribay 1991, 119-133). Under the direction of Gürsel, the *Milli Birlik Komitesi* (Committee of National Unity) was organized to form a new constitution to accommodate the advent of a Turkish multiparty system; address political and social Islamic issues; adopt measures to correct the economic budget deficit; and prepare for a coalition to rescue the reins of power from the care-taker military, interim government (Geyikdagi 1984, 137). Although civilian government was restored with a new constitution in 1961, General Gürsel remained as president until replaced by another General, Cevdet Sunay. Along with these generals, coalition governments were held together by İnönü until 1965 when a new party, the Justice Party (the resurrected Democratic Party of Bayar and Menderes), brought Süleyman Demirel to power. Dissatisfaction with the Justice party continued until the military issued an ultimatum for Demirel's resignation in 1971. Before the coup of 1971, the military had regularly insisted on public order because of social discontent and political terrorism. These problems intensified during Demirel's regime as an increasing awareness of economic and social gaps led to political terrorism and gang warfare.

After the military intervention in 1971, nonparty governments ruled until new elections were held in 1973. Terrorism and general public dissatisfaction continued, and parliament was so divided, it was unable to agree on a new president to replace Sunay. Political instability reigned along with deterioration of the economy until 1975. Then from 1975-80, Demirel and Ecevit alternately held together unsuccessful coalitions.

Turkey, since the foundation of the republic, had wrestled with many political, legal, social and economic problems. The Atatürk reforms had transformed an Islamic empire into a secular republic, completed by the adoption of the Swiss Civil Code. This legal transformation was the most radical of the reforms, because it represented the erosion of fundamental Islamic law, the heart of the Muslim *umma*. The economic policy of etatism had been relatively successful until Bayar attempted to privatize some of the state industries. He also limited state control of the economy, causing another disruption in the new republic. The political responsibilities of transforming an Islamic state into a democratic republic required the capacity to form a two-party system to oppose the stronghold held by the Republican Peoples Party for more than twenty-seven years. That opposition party, the ill-fated Democrats led by Menderes and Bayar, ended with their arrests and Turkey's first military coup imposed by General Gürsel. This coup justified the expediency and the necessity not only for this first coup, but for subsequent coups designed to ensure the Atatürk legacy dedicated to strict separation of affairs of state from Islamic politicized movements. The social problems were principally responses by Islamic fundamentalists unwilling to subscribe to a radically transformed state.

## Military Tradition

The ever-present watch-dog status exercised by the military in Turkish politics has not been sufficiently accepted or understood by the western world when examining, measuring or evaluating factors promoting a democratized nation. Military heroes had led Turkey from 1923-1937; the republic was founded by the benevolent military dictator Atatürk and followed by the equally skillful military hero, İnönü. Thus for a period of fourteen years, the military heroes, respected by the mass populace voted for the one party (Republican Peoples Party), until an opposition party was elected in 1950 (Menderes and Bayar). The first military coup ten years later reflected the mantle of power vested in a self-appointed military force guaranteeing and enforcing the Atatürk legacy of the Turkish secular republic. During this coup, generals shared power with coalitions headed by İnönü until 1965. The second coup in 1971 had forced Demirel's resignation as a result of the government's inability to control terrorism and widespread dissatisfaction.

Foreign observers living in Turkey during these coups were and are concerned with what seems to be overt expressions of a nation established by military fiat; the officers have been reluctant to relinquish power to non-military, elected officials, even after stability seems to have been restored. This observation is based upon three coups from 1960-1980, as well as the threat of a fourth coup, had not Necmettin

Erbakan resigned in 1997. These observations are also supported by the reluctance of the European Union to grant Turkey full admission beyond customs union status until the 1999 membership candidacy status. The rationale for this EU decision was based on several factors which included coups and extended military rule. The foregoing background information assists in explaining the establishment of Turkey by military heroes and the two military coups prior to the 1980 coup. Although the time-frame for this book is 1980-1998, the foregoing discussion of the previous coups and military activities provide a partial raison d'etre for the 1980 coup.

An important precedent established in the 1960 coup was the protection of corporate interests held by military officers. After the 1960 coup, the Army Mutual Assistance Foundation became a major holding company with one of its subsidiaries (Renault assembly plant) representing Turkey's third largest foreign investment (from the 1960s to the 1980s). The association of military personnel with major industrial enterprises continued during General Evren's presidency in 1980-83 (Rustow 1987, 129). Another economic factor directly related to the military is the more than six hundred thousand conscripted military forces Turkey has consistently maintained. The Ministry of National Defense, responsible for the conscription of every male Turkish citizen over the age of eighteen for one and one-half years of service, is Turkey's largest contractor and employer. Since the usual Turkish family has at least one or more sons who must serve in the military, it is a central part not only of Turkish society, but also of the political heritage from Atatürk to Evren.

Atatürk set a precedent not always followed by subsequent military figures. He mobilized urban, rural, Islamic and secular civilian opinions and insisted on the separation of the military from political affairs and Islam from government affairs. The Republican People's Party was established from civilian, local organizations. Atatürk's successor, İsmet İnönü, made the decision in 1948 to implement Atatürk's populist principles by recommending an opposition party to oppose his Republican People's Party. This opposition party, the Democratic Party under Bayar and Menderes, as previously discussed, ended when the 1960 military coup convicted Menderes and other party members of crimes against the republic, for which Menderes was hanged. These military actions were not in the tradition of Atatürk's vision for the republic. Moreover, these militant actions against the Bayar and Menderes administration blocked attempts by those seriously engaged in building the structures for a democratic system based on a multi-party concept.

Again, Atatürk's vision for a democratic republic was weakened by the "coup by memorandum" from 1971-73. During this coup the generals seized power, and forced the appointment of a non-party cabinet that met with their approval. The military also acted against the extremists in the major provinces. From 1971-75, nonpartisan cabinets under five different acting prime ministers held together care-taker governments approved by the military until Demirel was appointed as prime minister in 1975. The military in Turkey holds a unique sociopolitical status in which it is simultaneously revered and feared by each segment of society. The military is immediately recognized as the heir to the secular legacy Atatürk established for the reformed, enlightened Turkish Republic. Comprised of a vanguard of well-educated officers (serious guardians of the secular foundations of Atatürk's reforms), the military is a stabilizing, enduring and cohesive unit. The military quelled the violent riots of the late 1979-80 period; and after the 1980 coup, General Evren officiated in the political capacity as president. The precedent of the military, as guardian of the secular republic, had been established by Atatürk, was dominant in the 1960 and 1971 coups, and prevailed for a three-year period in the 1980 coup. Subsequent to each coup, the military was instrumental in the planning and drafting of each new constitution. This involvement with the drafting of each new constitution may be interpreted as conciliatory in terms of understanding Atatürk's intentions to retain Islam as the religion of the people, while maintaining and continuing a secularized government structure. In other words, the military is usually monitoring the sections of the constitution dealing with the establishment of new parties and any attempts to resurrect previous Islamic affiliated parties or religious training schools.

Mobilizing the political structure and civilians became a function of the military. Political conditions under Bayar and Menderes as previously cited, necessitated military intervention in the 1960 coup. Conversely, however, during the interim period before İsmet İnönü became president in 1961, the military generals appeased the political conservatives in the promotion of Islam by allocating state resources to reinstitute the Iman-hatip schools for Islamic training. When the secular bureaucracy was staffed with some of the graduates from these Imam-hatip schools, the military realized the inconsistencies and conflicts inherent in their attempts to fulfill the dictates of the secular state while simultaneously addressing the Turkish Islamic identity crisis by appeasing the political conservatives (Ahmad 1993, 221).

The interim 1960-1961 period was a time when military officials and the political conservatives had resurrected Islamic concerns. These concerns and issues continued to be utilized for political gain by certain parties with Islamic affiliation that appealed to a broad segment of society. Two forces, the military and the Islamic actors, have assumed roles as interventionists, policy innovators, recreators of Islamic identity and governmental care-takers in each critical political phase since the first coup.

The election of December 1995 was one of the more recent examples of peaceful military intervention when the formation of a coalition government between Erbakan's Islamic Welfare Party and Tansu Çiller's True Path Party became necessary. The secular status of the military, in addition to the 1980 constitutional dictates forbidding an Islamic party, could have been justification for rejecting Erbakan's voter election lead over Çiller. Detailed points of legalese could have buried the issue since the official title is Welfare Party rather than Islamic Welfare Party (used to identify Islamic affiliation). After less than a year in office Erbakan resigned rather than permit military intervention. Western observers are critical of the self-appointed political power delegated to the military in their dedication to upholding the secular status of the Atatürk legacy. Turkey's military legacy is uncontested; however, the *raison d'etre* for military intervention during government crises has been contested as unrepresentative of democratic stable government according to criteria established for EU membership. Despite external EU evaluative criteria for political stability, and OECD recommendations for transforming the economy, the military coup of 1980 disrupted civilian rule.

# The 1980 Coup

On September 12th, 1980, General Kenan Evren led a bloodless coup to restore the democratic principles upon which Atatürk had established the republic. To demonstrate the seriousness of the inability of Demirel's government to cope with unchecked political and economic instability, General Evren and part of his army rolled tanks through the streets of major cities. He and his staff declared a peaceful seizure of executive and legislative power; censored the press; imposed martial law on the sixty-seven provinces; assumed control of the political par-

ties; arrested one-hundred politicians; deposed the Demirel government; suspended the constitution; dissolved the Assembly and designated a cabinet led by Admiral Bülent Ülüsü. Several factors precipitated this third coup: the ongoing trade deficit; inflation reaching
one-hundred-twenty-seven percent by 1980; general social tension; underground violence; conflicts between the Islamic Sunni majority and
the Shiite minority; and the inability of any political party to gain a
majority. Underground violence, and socially and politically polarized
groups that protested against the secular structure of the Turkish republic resulted in more than five thousand deaths (Rustow 1987, 57-64).

This military-led government from 1980-83 enacted legislation by
passing or rejecting bills that had been ignored during the crises and
had paralyzed the state. An advisory council worked on a new constitution and assigned the care-taker government the responsibility of
monitoring and controlling political activity as well as limiting citizen
freedom to organize groups. Two years after the coup, a new constitution was finally drafted and approved by voters; a year later, by the
end of 1983, a civilian parliament and cabinet were installed. Although
a civilian parliament was installed, the 1982 constitution made provisions for General Evren to serve as president for seven years. This
constitution had been drafted by a civilian assembly and convened by
military generals. This new constitution theoretically supported
multiparties (see constitution, part two, articles 68 and 69, Appendix
II) by referring to parties as "indispensable elements of the democratic
political system." Rustow, however, refers to an "accompanying electoral law" which supported a two-party system." His position reflects a
western democratic bias that a stable Turkish government, supported
by two or more parties, would have increased capacity to deal with
political and economic difficulties in comparison with the "deadlocked
coalition cabinets of the 1960s and 1970s." The rationale for a stron-
ger government, measured by a workable balance between the president and a cabinet responsible to the Grand National Assembly, would
undoubtedly out-perform the unstable coalitions prior to the 1980 coup
(Rustow 1987, 59-60). The military, however, attempted to control the
direction of future political parties by selecting party leaders for the
1983 election.

How could any civilian political system function after General Evren
had gained control of the political parties and had removed from office
Prime Minister Süleyman Demirel and the opposition leader, Bülent
Ecevit? Would a non-military party emerge and gain support sufficient

to off-set the control of political parties exercised by the military during the 1980-1983 period? Part of the answer to these questions were contained in the care-taker quasi-military led government (through the National Security Council) from 1980-1983. In preparation for restoration to a civilian government, the generals preferred political candidates (specifically the offices of prime minister and president) not affiliated with the administration prior to the 1980 coup. Another answer to the question of the restoration of civilian government seemed to be contained within the new *Anavatan Partisi*/ANAP (Motherland Party) led by Turgut Özal. This party (ANAP) had adopted policies favored by the National Security Council and the military. Moreover, only parties approved by the NSC were allowed to run in the election set for November of 1983. The ANAP party won the election and parliament selected Özal as prime minister. Although the military controlled the government for a three-year period, the test of its dedication to restoring the reigns of power to civilian rule occurred during this time-frame. The military favored the new Nationalist Democracy Party; but in 1983, Özal's party, unaffiliated with the military, was voted into power.

During the period of military rule from 1980-83, the tenets of Atatürk's secular republic were expected to be reinforced; however, the NSC permitted Islamic schools to reopen. Consequently, when the guardians of Kemalist secularism were preoccupied with designing a new government, Islamic institutions were allowed to operate. As a result of this dual policy of secularism and Islamism, state support for Islamic education continued under the ANAP led by Özal. Moreover, as an appeasement to the mass populace, state support for Islamic education seemed to be a method for Özal to remain in power (first as prime minister and then as president) from 1983 until 1991 (Ahmad 1993, 750-769).

# Restoration to Civilian Government under Turgut Özal

Although Özal was accepted by the NSC and the military as a new candidate, he did not come to the office of prime minister without experience or service to the Turkish government in economic capacities. Perhaps Özal's most important contribution was his constructive efforts to transform Turkey's economy from etatism to a free market system. In 1950, the Mendres government had attempted an unconstructive change from etatist to private enterprise. Lacking in economic knowledge, his efforts resulted in excessive imports without an adequate balance of payment structure. A free market economy set the stage for abandoning import-substitution policies. Özal, the author of the 1980 Economic Liberalization Program, promoted Turkey's advancement into exporting semi-competitive industrial products. During Özal's service as prime minister, Turkey experienced a six to eight percent growth rate among the Organization for Economic Cooperation and Development members. Özal, a former World Bank consultant from 1971-1973, was also responsible for modern banking procedures and convertible currency policies (OECD reports 1986-1990).

Özal's foreign policy measures included: closing pipelines from Iraq to Turkey after the 1990 invasion of Kuwait; promotion of Turkish membership in NATO; developing trade relations with Central Asia (principally the Turkic Republics of the former USSR); and promotion of the Black Sea Economic Cooperative and the EU customs union. He was an example of a secular leader who could balance his dedication to the economic and political advancement of Turkey with his devout Islamic beliefs. Özal believed that the more prosperous nations should assist the masses in the less developed nations through constructive endeavors. His visionary ideas held objectives for the millennium based upon freedom, progress, prosperity and peace.

Özal's three basic freedoms of thought, conscience and religion were published posthumously *(Değişim Belgeleri* [Documents on Change] in 1993). These documents also contained guidelines for Turkey's transition from etatism to a free-market economy as well as plans for the creation of infrastructures, the reorganization and decentralization of government, how to amend the constitution, and plans for educational changes and health service. In another one of his publications, *La Turquie en Europe* (Turkey in Europe), Özal discussed Turkey's glorious past when the Ottoman Empire significantly contributed to Europe. His underlying objective for writing this book seemed to be focused on elucidating the ideas that Europe did not harbor prejudices against Turkey; both nations had positively interacted; and Turkey's 1987 request for EU membership had substantial support.

His concepts to plot Turkey's continual modernization course both economically and politically were not in conflict with his *Sufi* Islamic beliefs or even his active involvement in the Organization of the Islamic Conference. He had been the only successful Turkish politician capable of separating his Islamic beliefs from the affairs of state. However, a case could be made that subsequent political leaders attempting to revitalize Islam were influenced by Özal's unmatched success in both the political and the religious spheres. Özal was a member of the *Nakshibendi dervish* order. Intellectuals, professors and various levels of Turkish society have found solace in *Sufism* as an expression of Islam, seemingly compatible with secularization. The perspectives of the founder, Beduzzaman Said Nursi (1876-1960), accommodated western technology and knowledge with the practiced tenets of Islam, seemingly without the polarization of either (Tapper 1994, 133).

# Coalition Governments from 1991-1996

After Özal's sudden death in 1991, Demirel was elected as president and Tansu Çiller, leader of the new True Path Party (DYP) became prime minister. Again, a new party with a new name (True Path Party) had its roots in a former party denied legitimacy as a result of the military coup of 1980. What seemed to have happened with this DYP was a situation in which the old Menderes Democratic Party, after the 1960 coup, assumed the title Justice Party. Then after the 1980 coup, this same party subsequently divided into three or even four splinter groups with differing party agendas defined by their separate leaders. Özal's ANAP was one of the splinter groups finally accepted by the military. The military had encouraged the election of the new Nationalist Democracy Party; however, voters were seemingly interested in a candidate who campaigned without military credentials. The military accepted Özal's 1983 election victory; and the officers submitted the reigns of power to the new leader. Meanwhile, the DYP, another wing of the splintered group (Democratic and Justice), awaited its opportunity. This opportunity did not occur until 1991, because the military had delegitimized all political parties and held them responsible for what they (the military) had pronounced as close to civil war. This civil war situation had been sufficient rationale for the 1980 coup. Thus the ANAP (Motherland Party) had the opportunity to exercise political power through its leader Özal while the other party (DYP) from similar origins was confronted with establishing its legitimacy.

Opportunity for the DYP was realized in the 1989 local elections when there was evidence of fragmentation in the ANAP. This fragmentation of the party in power seemed to stem from a credibility issue based upon the ANAP's ideological support for a free-market economy, yet the administration expanded the state's role (etatism) in economic issues. Despite the negligible election gain, the DYP led by Tansu Çiller failed to integrate its party platform with liberal free-market economics or the ability to compromise. The point is that the ANAP did not have a leader comparable to Özal, yet the DYP (even in the absence of a strong successor to the ANAP) seemed incapable of assuming the ambitious liberal free-market agenda undertaken by Özal and his party. Further, economic globalization was precipitated by liberalized economic measures on a global scale more readily adopted by developed nations than developing or less-developed states. Therefore, Turkey, a developing state was caught in a situation in the 1980s in which economic reform took precedence over political capability (see OECD chapter). Political capability and growth of democratic processes had been impeded by military intervention and coups which delegitimized political parties. These political parties in their efforts to reestablish and legitimize themselves had to adopt new identities, names and agendas; gain political skills necessary for forming a substantial party base; and learn negotiation skills necessary to form coalitions based on compromise.

One serious fault in Turkish party formation can be identified as the persistent issue of internal democratization. The problem is that each party is regulated by its leader; no real internal democratized party structure with shared powers seems to exist; and there has been limited expression of party members acting autonomously from their leaders. Another party problem relates to external pressures from economic organizations and development groups examining the level of democratic procedures prevalent in the system of Turkish government. Thus some candidates become identified with Turkish political parties attempting to implement new policies and establish party platforms associated with these external economic groups.

Demirel, who became president of Turkey when Özal died in office, had been representative of Turkish politicians identifying with concepts of democratization. He attempted to place the military under civilian control through a proposed constitutional bill. This bill, had it passed, would have placed the general chief of staff under the Minister of Defense. Continuing with attempts to democratize Turkey's political structures he introduced the issue of human rights around 1991. In a publication of Özal's speeches, he stated that "Turkey must accept universal values; whatever the charter for the Conference on Security and Cooperation in Europe entails, Turkey must adjust its legal and constitutional order to it" (*Değişim Belgeleri* 1993, 14).

Demirel's position for Turkey was organized around democratization, welfarism and human rights, whereas Çiller, a member of the same DYP, emphasized a separation of a market economy from political liberalism, enhancing a conservative populist ideology (moving the DYP from a centrist position to the right) and identifying with the military position during Kurdish uprisings. Although Çiller advocated privatization of the SEEs and discussed market liberalization as an economic objective, she moved the party to the right of the former central position in an effort to separate her policies from Demirel. This effort was reinforced by aligning the DYP with the National Action Party (radical right) in an effort to gain strength against the Islamic Welfare Party, a serious competitor of all so-called rightist parties. Moreover, Çiller's efforts were also against Demirel, one of her own party members who advocated policies in opposition to her popularized and growing faction within the same True Path Party/DYP (Sakallioglu 1996,142-157).

## Government Structure Post-1996

The December 1996 election ended with three parties (*RP*, ANAP and DYP) forming another coalition government. The distribution of votes probably came as no surprise to Turkey, but the western world seemed concerned that the winner in this coalition was a former Islamic party led by Necmettin Erbakan. The *Refâh Partisi* (Welfare Party) had changed its name and had prepared for elections in order to hold seats in parliament. While the military had been preoccupied with closing down all political parties after the 1980 coup, including two formerly legitimized Islamic parties, inconsistencies in maintaining secular policies abounded. Not only had Islamic institutions flourished during the military period from 1980-1983, but the former Islamic parties simply united forces and emerged as one party under the name *Refâh Partisi*. This same party had returned to competitive politics in 1983 with an entirely different party platform from that of its former Islamic parties.

The earlier Islamic parties had supported economic growth and development in Turkey. However, with the 1980 shift to a free-market export-oriented economy, the new Welfare Party declared industry to be against its mainstream supporters. These mainstream traditional supporters were primarily small businesses producing for internal markets. The Islamic party's previous emphasis had focused on economic development, but later shifted to a criticism of the world economic order and capitalism. Capitalism, according to the Welfare Party, integrates Turkey's economy with world markets and Israeli military objectives. Therefore, the Welfare Party reinforced the former Islamic party's concept of the world economy as destructive to Islamic society. The Welfare Party refers to world economy as the slave order (*köle düzen*). Their objective is to rescue Turkey from the world economy through its just order (*adil düzen*). This just order according to Islamist belief, includes an economic system comprised of a common market of Muslim countries, a common currency, no taxes and no interest charged by banks (Toprak 1983, 413-415). The *Refâh Partisi* is reportedly supported by the *Rabit'at al-Alam al-Islami*, the Saudi-based world Islamic organization. This organization advocates the return of an Islamic state by denying the secularized state institutionalized by Atatürk. This party is noted for establishing a community elan similar to the concept of the Islamic *umma*. This spirit of community is achieved by party members who are active in assisting villagers who migrate to Turkish cities in pursuit of work, and in gaining international assistance for alienated Turkish immigrant workers in Europe (Mehmet 1990, 124).

During the first three months in office, Erbakan as prime minister seemed intent on forming coalitions and reassuring the West that his party would adhere to agreements formerly negotiated. Although the new government was carefully monitored by the military, no objection was registered when the new prime minister entered into a coalition with Çiller establishing her as the new foreign minister. After this coalition, Erbakan additionally reassured the West that the customs union clinched in 1995 during Çiller's administration as prime minister would continue on course with some modifications. After Erbakan began a series of discussions with Arab leaders, his focus seemed to be strongly identified with the Middle East rather than identification with the West and renewing the request for membership in the EU (New York Times 07-12-96, A 8). He began advocating the *Refâh Partisi* objectives of a Middle East customs union and trade negotiations between Turkey and the Arab nations. As this dialogue progressed his position was threatened by the military until his forced resignation in 1997. After less than a year as prime minister, Erbakan apparently realized that his policies were not acceptable to the watch-dog military; that the alternative seemed to be another military intervention or his resignation. Selecting the latter of the two alternatives, the Turkish government was once again thrust into assembling a temporary government until a declared election could be held. Thus for a period of approximately seven months, the coalition with the second highest number of votes (Yilmaz, leader of Özal's ANAP) maintained government until Prime Minister Bülent Ecevit was appointed by President Demirel in 1999.

The April 1999 elections were no surprise as far as voters' expressions for a party leader whose reputation has remained untainted by political scandals: Ecevit, a seasoned politician and leader of the Democratic Left Party (DSP), received the greatest percentage of votes. However, one of the parties of the coalition government receiving the second highest number of votes was a surprise: the National Movement Party (MHP), a rightist, ultra-nationalistic party formerly known as the Grey Wolves who were held responsible for some of the violence during the 1970s; and they were also known for their opposition to Ecevit's policies during the beginning of his political career in 1974. The third highest votes were cast for Özal's Motherland Party now led by Yilmaz and the Islamic Virtue Party. When Erbakan resigned from office in 1997, his *Refâh Partisi* was dissolved; however, it surfaced again in 1999 under the new name of the Virtue Party. After only three months in office, Prime Minister Ecevit demonstrated his political skills in dealing with the coalition formed from the above-mentioned parties. With cooperation from the opposition parties, Ecevit engineered through parliament long-standing issues relating to acceptance of direct foreign investment; passage of legislation formerly recommended by the International Monetary Fund; overdue large-scale privatization of the SEEs; and internal issues related to social security, retirement and health care (Wall Street Journal 8-16-99, A10; also, OECD chapter). Although Ecevit faced opposition from his coalition government, he and President Demirel apparently shared similar views regarding Turkey's march toward modernization, democratization and identity with the EU (the customs union and now candidacy status for membership in the European Union).

Demirel and Ecevit, although representing different party identities (Demirel DYP, Ecevit DSP), shared power during Turkey's difficult years from 1975 until the 1980 coup. Their former parties, the Democratic, then the Justice Party, were banned with the military coup of 1980. The Justice Party splintered; it emerged in 1983 as three different parties with two currently legal and actively engaged in Turkey's political processes (the DYP and the DSP). President Demirel had begun his political career as prime minister in 1965 and was successively reelected until 1971 when the military forced his resignation. This forced resignation occurred as a result of general public dissatisfaction with his policies, terrorist actions and his defiance of the military as policy formulators. Uncontrolled terrorist actions waged against the govern-ment were terminated by the military coup of 1971. Then in 1975 the Justice Party, by forming a coalition, ushered Demirel to power as prime minister. Thus from 1975 until the 1980 coup, Demirel and Ecevit, through weak coalitions, held the government together. The govern-ment agenda approved by Demirel included possible nuclear energy power; foreign-built gas-fired electricity plants; controlled inflation plans from the IMF; plans for thirty to forty billion in foreign investment and continued privatization of the SEEs. Continuing with his former de-mocratization ideas, Demirel confirmed Turkey's official acceptance as a candidate for membership in the EU. "Turkey is determined to rid itself of the poor human-rights record and undemocratic methods that have discouraged investors." (Wall Street Journal 2-16-2000, A23).

# Turkish Women as Exponents
# of the Islamic Parties

Atatürk's reforms granted women educational opportunities unattain-able prior to 1995. The response to those opportunities established women in professional positions other than political. Tansu Çiller, ap-pointed prime minister in 1993 was the first woman serving in this capacity. Çiller could be considered as a role model for women who became active in the 1995 campaign; however, their support was fo-cused on an Islamic party. In 1995 when the *Refâh Partisi* (now Virtue Party or *Fazilat Partisi*) propelled Erbakan to power, Turkish women identifying with this party were actively engaged in the campaign pro-cess. According to the *Turkish Daily News,* women's participation in the *Refâh Partisi*'s efforts to secure new members and votes was a decisive contribution. Women *Refâh Partisi* members were also active in assisting families migrating from villages to cities (Turkish Daily News 10-9-95, A3). The *Refâh Partisi* created a cadre of voter support and established a community spirit identified with the Islamic *umma* (community of believers). This party seemingly possessed the skill to involve women for the purpose of promoting their political agenda without awarding them power positions within the party. The *Refâh Partisi* was one of the most visibly identifiable movements within revi-talized Islam. Businesses cognizant of Islamic movements created spe-cial apparel for women indicating their traditional or political stance. Headdresses referred to as *basortu* were worn by women adhering to traditional Islamic practices. This group represented women not necessarily anti-Atatürk, but older women not actively involved in the Atatürk modernizing phase. Within the past decade, university students identified with the Islamic movement have elected to wear headdresses symbolizing a political, even militant commitment to revitalized Islam (Kadioğlu 1996).

Admittedly the Atatürk reforms did not present a series of options to women who were thrust into secularized society and asked to forsake the traditional dress and veil. They were asked to westernize, to Europeanize, to adopt western style clothing, to learn to read and write and to become educated. The traditional village women, reluctant to adopt the western attire, remained steadfast in their Islamic beliefs unless confronted with external and/or internal reasons for change. If they migrated to the cities on a somewhat permanent basis, gradually they modified their attire to meet the demands of the work force. Thus the Atatürk reforms presented only two options: the nationalized secularized women, or the women who refused to comply with the reforms.

These two options polarized society for Turkish women in the political, social and economic sectors by marginalizing the village women and creating educational opportunities for those women joining the ranks of Atatürk's reforms. Politically, women living in cities and identifying with the reforms joined the ranks of Atatürk's political party and party successors. Conversely, conservative Islamic and village women remained steadfastly identified with the political ideology of Islamic law, the *umma* (community of believers) and the teachings of the Koran. Women who identified with the reform movement temporarily lost their Islamic identity when they qualified for professional positions. The conservative and village women maintained their Islamic identity, which resulted in limited change, unless they migrated or emigrated to cities in pursuit of work. Economically, the women identifying with the reformist movement began joining the ranks of males enrolling in academic schools in preparation for professional careers. Slowly, the conservative Islamic women who left the villages for work became aware of the necessity to read and write—to become educated to the extent that they could apply for a job and conduct monetary exchanges and purchases. Thus the problem for Turkish women from the outset of the Atatürk reforms initiated in 1923, continued to be the gap between the two poles (the secularists and the Islamic conservatives).

Women who had joined the secular reforms disaggregated themselves not only from their former Islamic status, but also from the women who remained steadfast in Islam. This social gap, this disaggregation of Turkish women, was the beginning of two separate classes: the educated westernized socially secure employed women, and those who remained Islamic conservatives (resigned to agrarian village work or migratory, low-wage work in large cities). This social as well as economic gap continued to create cleavages in Turkish society with limited attempts to close the gaps until the resurgence of Islamic movements in the 1980s. These movements, while involving women in social and political issues, have not alleviated the increasing economic distance between the two classes. Moreover, the resurgence or revitalization of Islam as a social and political movement has created a third gap among the educated and uneducated.

Since Islamic society strives for equality and social justice, indeed there is considerable ideological conflict between the social classes of the secular educated women; the educated Islamic women; and the uneducated Islamic women. Although Islam seemingly unites two groups of women with different perspectives, the social and economic inequalities prevent recognition of the complete interpretation of Islamic social justice. The traditional Islamic perspectives prior to the Atatürk reforms remain steadfast; however, the Islamic resurgence identified with the1980s attempted to reconcile two areas. Those two areas were the private and public lives of women who wore Islamic head-gear and dress (representing the private life) into the public work place. This symbolism was an attempt to demonstrate not only adherence to Islamic values, but also to exercise power in the public domain. This exercise of power through attire was a defiant expression by those educated Muslim women well aware of the ban on Islamic dress (Arat 1997, 256-257).

These Islamic women identifying themselves by special attire are members of the Virtue Party (*Fazilat Partisi*). In the April 1999 Turkish parliament election, Merve Kavakci from Istanbul was elected as a Virtue Party member. When the swearing-in-to-office ceremony occurred, Kavakci was asked to leave because she appeared in *hijab* (Islamic headgear). The voters who elected Kavakci knew her identity from the campaign trail. Despite President Demirel's insistence that no *hijab* would be allowed in parliament, Kavakci insisted that wearing the *hijab* was her right and duty. Secularists have applied to the constitutional court for banning the Virtue Party.[4]

The Islamic Virtue Party, as previously mentioned, emerged after the government banned Erbakan's *Refâh Partisi* in 1998. Precursors to the *Refâh Partisi* were the National Order Party banned in 1971 and the

National Salvation Party banned in 1980. As previously discussed, a number of parties in Turkey with a history of conflicts with the military or the government, restructured by meeting the constitutional criteria for forming a new party. The reemergence of Muslim affiliated parties is predicated on the assumption that a determined number of citizens are dedicated to advancing the principles of Islam in the social, economic and political dimensions. Among this group are those who wish to see Islamic social values advanced without disrupting the secular foundations or a return to an Islamic state. There are also those considered as radicals who advocate a state in which economic interests are aligned with other Islamic nations, a plan proposed by former Prime Minister Erbakan and his *Refâh Partisi*. Erbakan envisioned Turkey as the leader of an economic organization similar to the EU, but limited to Muslim nations. The *Refâh Partisi* supported an economic policy advocating the Islamic principles of social justice. This economic policy did not comply with either capitalism or socialism, because the objective was to end dependency upon external forces other than Islamic states. When Erbakan was confronted by political and military opposition, implementing his vision of Turkey as the leader of an Islamic economic organization became unrealistic. The fourth possible military intervention was avoided by Erbakan's resignation in 1997.

Despite the impediments to secularization, modernization and economic growth, the nascent and at times divided republic (Islamic versus secular division) has persevered. Gradual economic measures recommended by external and internal organizations and groups have catapulted Turkey from a less-developed state to a developing republic. Turkey's secular Prime Minister Ecevit and President Demirel have cooperatively engaged in economic progress as witnessed by the August 1999 passage and approval of legislation recommended by the International Monetary Fund, the OECD and Turkish economists. Ecevit's skills in garnering support from his opposition parties and the parliamentary coalition to accomplish the passage of legislation (as well as its approval by President Demirel) also indicate progressive steps toward relative government stability. These cooperative political endeavors bode well with the European Union as Turkey continues to be evaluated for membership after having reached candidacy status. According to the 2006 EU Commission Progress Report, Turkey continues to meet political and economic conditions. The May, 2007 threat to political stability has been partially settled by the court system recommending that Prime Minister Recep Erdoğan select another candidate for president. Mass demonstrations against his Islamic affiliated party, and the selection of Abdullah Gül for president, erupted in major cities throughout Turkey.

## Conclusion for Chapter Three

Turkey's transformation from an Islamic state to a republic was a process marked by political, social and economic upheaval. The comprehensive reforms instituted at the beginning of 1923 by Turkey's military hero, Atatürk, resulted from exposure and interaction with Europe and the West. Adoption of the Swiss Civil Code of Law was the most radical reform measure to be accomplished by a nation imbued with Islamic law. Supplementing the Turkish legal system with concessions to non-Muslim inhabitants during the Ottoman Empire had regularly occurred before 1923; however, abolishing the *Şeriat* disestablished Islamic family law. Application of the new civil code tested the capacity of the courts: as a vehicle for the dissemination of information regarding the Swiss Civil Code; to interpret the new legal system; and to integrate Islamic family law into the Swiss Civil Code.

Although a republic had been established, Turkey had been governed for twenty-seven years by benevolent military heroes representing only one party (*Chumhuriyet Halk Partisi* [Republican People's Party]). The multiparty concept was introduced as late as 1950 and enacted that year in the election of the first opposition party to the Republican People's Party. This opposition party, the Democratic Party, through lack of political experience, incompetence and corruption, precipitated the first military coup in 1960. A subsequent military "coup by memorandum" from 1971-73, although less militant, retarded the processes of government stability as perceived by the endogenous political structure, the mass populace, and exogenous organizations. Generals who led the bloodless 1980 coup cooperated with civilian government officials in revising the 1980 constitution. Officials of the 1980 coup, through constitutional revisions, attempted to dissolve political parties classified as corrupt, ineffective or Islamic affiliated. However, the new parties entering the political arena in the officially held 1983 election had roots in the formerly banned parties. Concepts of economic liberalization affected the quality of political democracy with the advent of Özal's government after the 1980 coup. During Özal's administration opposition parties were honing their skills in groups that emerged as factions of the Democratic center and right. Since 1960 the number of political parties has increased to the extent that garnering sufficient voter support for any one party has become proportional to the need for the leading party to form a coalition government.

From the beginning of the republic to the present, the parliamentary government has grappled with issues that could have caused the termination of civilian government by the military. The observant outsider concludes that the military is all-powerful and in control when a state crisis occurs. However, high-ranking military officials inform those observers that the political function of the military is to guard the secular status of the republic; that after a crisis is perceived to be under control and government stability has been restored, the military retreats. Irrespective of the external or internal perception of the role of the military in the political arena, the republic as a whole has grappled with a series of serious issues affecting government stability. These issues have included the transformed political, legal, economic and social structures from Islamic to secular; three military coups precipitated by crises calling forth Atatürk's military legacy dedicated to safeguarding the secular republic; the threat of Islamic affiliated parties gaining control and reestablishing an Islamic state; the political skills required by party leaders to operationalize coalition governments; and similar political skills needed to pass parliamentary legislation for economic and political improvement.

This chapter has indicated that external foreign influence was apparent during the mixed religious and secular capitulatory court system; that exogenous influences were seemingly ignored during the Menderes/Bayar period; but that the effects of a third military coup (although bloodless) registered an awakening to external factors influential in Turkey's political and economic affairs. Even as an isolated factor, the 1980 coup was a denouement to the European awakening that influenced the Özal government following this coup. Aware of the Atatürk legacy, and concerned with Turkey's failed attempts to join the EU, Özal published materials discussing the importance of European and Turkish cooperation. He addressed the OECD recommendations for privatization of the SEEs and the requirements for the EU customs union. Under Özal's leadership Turkey experienced a redirection of its economic policies by responding to the necessity to survive in the interdependent globalized markets.

The millennium brought Turkey closer to its long awaited goal of EU membership now that candidacy status has been achieved. Prior to 2000, economic improvements in terms of EU evaluations seemed to have surpassed Turkey's human rights record, or the capacity to consistently maintain relative government stability without military intervention. Those economic improvements, however, were reversed during the years from 2000 to 2002 when the economy experienced difficulties. This economic slump caused voter dissatisfaction with Ecevit and Demirel. Thus the 2002 election ushered in Erdoğan as the leader of the Justice and Development party (AKP).

# Notes

1. The *Tanzimat* (act of giving new order to the state) was the official name given to a series of social and political reforms designed to modernize the vast Ottoman Empire (Albania, northern and eastern Greece, Crete, Serbia, Bosnia, Bulgaria, Rumania, Syria, Iraq, Jordan, Saudi Arabia, Egypt and Libya). Beginning in the latter half of the eighteenth century, the *Tanzimat* reforms targeted the military by establishing a school of military engineers. The *Tanzimat* reforms guaranteed that Muslims and non-Muslims would be granted equal rights and obligations with regard to military service, administration of justice, taxation, public employment and admission to educational institutions. Additional reforms included consultative and judicial bodies and the codification of civil law (see Resat Kaynar, *Mustafa Resit Pasa ve Tanzimat*. Ankara, 1954).

2. The *Mecelle* (a digest of legal rules and principles) represented the first attempt to codify Islamic civil law beginning in the early half of the nineteenth century. It was a compendium of sixteen books based on Islamic jurisprudence. It differed from traditional *shari'ah* Islamic law in terms of: codification, promulgation and admitting non-Muslims. The *Mecelle* also differed from European civil codes by omitting non-contractual obligations. Other than a section of the civil code based on French law, the Islamic *Mecelle* remained in force until the Swiss Civil Code replaced it in 1926 (see Ebul'ula Mardin, "Mecelle" in Islam Ansiklopedisi. Istanbul, 1940 and Charles Tyser, et al. The *Mecelle* Translated. Nicosia, 1901).

3. An excerpt from Atatürk's speech before the Faculty of Law on October 5, 1925: The Turkish Revolution signifies a transformation far broader than the word revolution suggests. . . . It means replacing an age-old political unity based on religion with one based on another tie, that of nationality. This nation has now accepted the principle that the only means of survival for nations in the international struggle for existence lies in the acceptance of the contemporary Western civilization. This nation has also accepted the principle that all of its laws should be based on secular grounds only, on a secular mentality that accepts the rule of continuous change in accordance with the change and develop-

ment of life's conditions as its law. . . . The time has come to lay the legal foundations and educate new men of law satisfying the mentality and needs of our revolution (full text quoted in Osman Ergin, *Turkiye Maarif Tarihi* (Istanbul, 1943), V. 1501-4; in Berkes 1964, *The Development of Secularism,* 470).

4. Vural Savas presided over the banning of the *Fazilat Partisi's* predecessor, the *Refâh Partisi* in January 1998. He applied to the constitutional court for closure of the *Fazilat* Partisi. This attempt will undoubtedly by contested by the *Fazilat Partisi* leader, Recai Kutan. Merve Kavakci, the elected official to Parliament from the Istanbul district, and a member of the *Fazilat Partisi,* became a spokesperson for the Islamic community not only in Turkey but in other Islamic nations. On May 8, 1999, several women students in Tehran protested the ban placed on Kavakci for wearing the *hijab* in Turkey's parliament (see Bangash, Zafar, "Turkey's Secular Fundamentalist Target," *Crescent International,* May 16-31, 1999 from http://www.inminds.com/hijab-ban/kavakci.htm).

# Chapter 4

## Turkey's State Capability Problems

### Introductory Remarks

These introductory remarks are related to the greater issues Turkey has faced as it transformed from an Islamic nation to a secular state. Specifically, what are the issue areas which have tested the capabilities and the effectiveness of the Turkish nation state? There is sufficient evidence that Turkey's continual quest and successful efforts to identify with Europe and the West discredit Huntington's "the classical torn country" concept. The dichotomy between Huntington's "torn state and core state" has no rational or substantive foundation. His basis for identifying Turkey as a "torn state" is predicated on the assumption that revitalized Islam prevents European and western identity and he reclassifies the republic as a "core state" rather than a torn or fragmented nation. Huntington describes Turkey as torn between its Islamic identity and westernization. According to Huntington's classificatory discretion of civilizations, Turkey should revert to a "core state" grouped with the Muslim Arab world (Huntington 1996, 137-140). His decision to classify Turkey as a "core state" within the Muslim Arab world is an arbitrary imputation assigned to unwilling nations.

First, Huntington's descriptive term, "core state" is assigned to Turkey on the basis of assumed leadership of the Muslim world. Huntington does not stand alone in his classificatory schema; however, others more knowledgeable in not only Turkish political affairs, but also the secularization of Turkey's institutions, have carefully examined revitalized Islam. Ozay Mehmet has classified his position for the reconciliation of revitalized Islam with Turkey's secular republic. He

has proposed the reinstitution of a modern version of the office of caliphate (the political and religious head of the Muslim world before
1924) solely for religious purposes. Turkey had assumed the role of
trustee of the caliphate for the whole of the Muslim world before Atatürk
abolished it in 1924. Mehmet acknowledges the fragmentation of Islam
as a result of the disestablishment of the caliph and the office of the
caliphate. He rationalizes that Turkey has a responsibility to reestablish
the central religious authority vested in the caliphate (Mehmet 1990,
232-233). He further rationalizes that a reestablished caliphate would
be recognized as universalizing and solidifying forces within Islam.[1]
Mehmet's position differs from Huntington's on the basis of accommodating Islam. Mehmet acknowledges that Turkey is a secular republic
under the rule of law with the capacity to accommodate political and
religious dissent. However, Huntington simply classifies Turkey as a
"torn state" with the capacity to become a "core state" by reuniting
with the Muslim world.

Huntington's work on civilizations (*The Clash of Civilizations and
the Remaking of World Order*) is important because it is the quintessen-
tial example of the lack of knowledge necessary to analyze Turkey's
institutional structures. This same publication is also an example of
extracting Turkey from its course of action in the world of nations by
arbitrarily assigning it to a bloc of Muslim nations analogous to forcing
a piece of the puzzle into a nonfitting space. A second issue related to
Huntington's use of the term "core state" is also important. He uses the
term to designate Turkey's possible role as the leader of the Muslim
world. His premise assumes that Turkey can become a "core state" by
removing itself from the "torn state" status (which it is not), and becoming reestablished in the Muslim world (again, moving a piece of
the world puzzle to posit it in a nonfitting area). For the sake of clarity,
Huntington's use of "core state" is completely unrelated to Wallerstein's
theoretical premise of the capitalist world divisions comprised of the
core, semiperiphery and periphery (see Appendix I).

Returning to the unwilling nations in Huntington's "torn or core
state," is the third issue. Turkey is unwilling to return to the former
status from which it has been separated since 1923. Moreover, the
Atatürk legacy of a secular Turkish nation has been maintained and at
times, enforced by the military. While maintaining a political republic
with a parliamentary system and an improved economy, Turkey has
continued to accommodate Islamic movements as it continues its secu-

larization processes. The remaining and also unwilling nations are those comprising the Arab Muslim world. The prospects that Turkey could become a Huntington "core state" (by assuming leadership of the Islamic world) are remote when considering Arab views of a secular nation state without an Islamic legal system. Moreover, the military and the current prime minister and president are dedicated to protecting the Atatürk legacy, and are persistently devoted to a secular political system and its identity with Europe and the West. Further, Turkey having reached the status of a state in the middle-income group of nations, has followed an arduous path to incremental growth. This path has been marked not only by sophisticated indices established by OECD, World Bank and other organization researchers examining economic growth in all countries, it is also marked by political development/stability and a participatory civil society.

Returning to the issue areas that have tested Turkey's capabilities and effectiveness, there have been at least six factors. Turkey has adjusted to three economic shifts, globalization and regionalization, external recommendations for political and economic development, the transformation processes, the military factor and the political balancing acts. Turkey's government has endured the three economic shifts as discussed in the OECD section; it has attempted to incorporate the exogenous recommendations from the World Bank, the OECD, the EU and others into functional policies. The acceptance and endurance of these economic shifts and recommendations have been fundamental preparation for Turkey's entry into regional and global markets. This entry into the regional and global markets has been facilitated by the recommendations and conditioning processes provided by the EU customs union as of 1995. Many of the recommendations have become policies as a result of the cooperative efforts and balancing acts of the Ecevit and Demirel administrations as they collaborated with the opposition in parliament. It seems that this state government capability exercised by Ecevit has been the cause for effective passable legislation. This political skill also demonstrates an understanding of the exercise of power and the democratic political process. Rather than cause a deadlock or discount the Islamic opposition Virtue Party, Ecevit catered to their requests and won their support for passage of legislation important to foreign investment in Turkey. Thus the capabilities and the effectiveness of the Turkish Republic have been demonstrated according to the criteria established by the World Bank.

The capabilities and effectiveness of states are critical in assisting businesses and firms in their understanding of global market opportunities. The global or world economy and its markets are increasingly referred to as globalization. Turkey, like other developing nations (classified by the World Bank as low-middle income states), contends with globalization and regionalization. For purposes of clarity, regionalization is defined as a process focused on the internal economic and political development of member nations working toward increased integration of their sovereignty. Globalization is defined as a process of economic external outreach at the macroeconomics level. Globalization, however, is a microeconomics phenomenon because it is principally driven by firms. These definitions are adaptations from the OECD conceptualization of globalization and regionalization (Osman 1994, 33-36).

These global firms function microeconomically, but they conduct trade at the macro level. Firms make decisions to maximize their profits in the capitalist market economy based on methods of production or technologies (Case and Fair 1996, 405). In developing countries vulnerable to the recommendations of external organizations, their firms may be subject to transitions. In other words, Turkey's state-owned enterprises have been slow in responding to the OECD recommended release of state-controlled enterprises and firms. From state control to private control, there may be changes in the combinations of capital, labor and technology during the transition period. This transition period may cause market fluctuations which may have adverse effects on the state government. As discussed in the OECD section of this book, Turkey experienced three shifts in its economic development efforts. The Keynesian era of government intervention, control and getting the "policies right," was replaced by the neo-classical economists focusing on trade liberalization and getting the "prices right." Thus during the 1980s and 1990s, Turkey was advised to privatize its State Economic Enterprises and develop export markets. Then at the beginning of the 90s, the World Bank began to focus on the distribution of labor between the state and markets. This idea was based on a cooperative working relationship between the state and the markets: If markets were efficient and productive, the state government should be non-interventionist; if markets were unproductive, the state government should carefully intervene. In the case with Turkey, the OECD plan was for privatization of the State Economic Enterprises, a slow reluctant process on the part of the Turkish parliament. Thus this plan required the Turkish parliament to approve legislation favoring the sell-offs of their state enterprises. In other words, planned intervention on the part of the state government to privatize industries was recommended by the OECD and the World Bank. This recommendation was based on the unproductive state-controlled enterprises. The World Bank's concern with the relationship between the state and markets was the beginning of its 1997 research project dedicated to state government capability and effectiveness (World Bank 1997, 41-61).

State governments, reluctant to enter the global economy, are confronted with the threat of being left out of the international trade processes and capital flows if they fail to join a regional trade group. Turkey, in its efforts to join the world economy, has held membership in the OECD since 1961; has been affiliated with the EU since 1963 (current customs union status; accepted as a candidate for membership on 12-11-99); and has qualified for World Bank loans. Many of the recommendations from the OECD, its affiliates and the EU have been implemented and are being considered by the Turkish parliament. These recommendations are designed to increase Turkey's overall growth and political/economic development.

The globalization process carries heavy responsibilities for all member states. This global integration is a collective action process in which member's actions have implications and consequences for other states. Member's actions are internationally interdependent; they become proportional to the growth of regional organizations. In other words, increased membership in the EU multiplies the collective action of states, and increases interdependence among nations and their responsibilities and cooperation with other nations. International cooperation and responsibilities can secure public goods and services otherwise not accessible.

In support of the theoretical perspectives and rationale for this book, if Turkey matches its micro-internal capabilities with government effectiveness, it is more likely to conduct macro-external cooperative relations with other organizations and nations in order to secure public goods and services. These international public goods and services at the global level rely on international cooperation without coercion. At this global interdependent level, voluntary support, rather than coercion, is the key mechanism for providing necessary public goods and services. These beneficial international public goods and services are world peace, a sustainable global environment, marketplaces for goods and services, and research knowledge (World Bank 1997, 131).

Collective action on the part of participating member nations in regional organizations is of course difficult. It requires an openness to the global economy and toleration of the diversity of different national standards. In order to facilitate this openness and diversity, functional regional and coordinating groups are necessary. The International Labor Organization and the Bank for International Settlements are functional groups with the capacity to cope with environmental protection, macroeconomics policies, labor standards and conflicts. The EU and other regional groups have the capacity to deal with various problems arising within their member nations, and the OECD has the ability to link the functional with the regional groups.

Turkey, with its OECD membership, extensive recommendations from the International Labor Organization for improved social security measures, and now a candidate for EU membership, seems to be in an advantageous position. Supported by internal government capacities and effectiveness, Turkey can promote and benefit from international public goods and services by continuing membership with the OECD, the EU candidacy status, and compliance with their recommendations. Additionally, assistance and recommendations from the ILO, the WTO, the World Bank and similar groups provide benefits to assist Turkey's continuous course of development and identity with Europe and the westernization processes.

The 1997 World Bank research revealed important information and rationale for focusing on international globalism and national pluralism rather than military security, referred to in international relations as realism. Their research reported that global military spending fell from four percent of the GDP in 1990 to two and seven-tenths percent in 1994 and four-tenths percent in 1995 (World Bank 1997, 140). This reduction in military spending resulted from the dissolution of the Soviet Union, an increase in global democratization and decreased military aid. Although Turkey falls within the percentage figures of the World Bank research, their military force remains strong and the capacity of the government to forge an alliance with Israel has been effective. On October 25, 1999, Turkey and Israel affirmed a military and economic alliance. This alliance, while alienating Turkey from the Arab world, strengthens its position in the unpredictable Middle East and reinforces incremental global democratization.

World Bank research supports the position that countries with membership in the OECD generally have state governments ranging from high to mid-level capabilities; that some of these nations have enacted the most comprehensive reforms possible (World Bank 1997, 167). State governments work for micro-internal pluralism and for macro-external globalization. Turkey represents a nation state with extensive reforms. As previously discussed, Atatürk and his cadre instituted sweeping political, economic and social reforms that transformed an Islamic nation into a secular republic in 1923, a process that continues to the present. Since 1923 the rule of law, one of the most critical changes for an Islamic nation, has remained the adopted and adapted Swiss Civil Code. Atatürk was advised by legal experts to adopt the Swiss Civil Code, considered to be one of the most modern western legal systems at that time. With the first requisite for a capable state adopted, the legal system, also compatible with European and western powers, Turkey had the beginnings of institution building. An institutionalized compatible legal system was considered foundational for the establishment of a responsible functional and accountable state.

The effectiveness and capabilities of the Turkish state have been tested from the time Ismet Inonu introduced a two-party system (initiated in 1950 when the opposition won the election), until the time of the military coups. The effectiveness and capabilities continue to be tested as a former Islamic state continues the processes of transformation, secularization, regionalization and globalization. From 1950 to the present, maintaining a secular state has been challenged by resurgent Islamic movements. Beginning with Inonu, political leaders have attempted flexible policies to accommodate Islamic groups clamoring for revitalized Muslim institutions. Subsequent to these concessions of accommodation, Islamic groups have misused the power gained by reestablishing Islamic institutions and political parties.

The 1982 constitutional provision forbidding the formation of Islamic parties caused the courts to eliminate the Welfare Party (an Islamic party) when it defied the military in 1996-97 (see constitution, part two, Articles 68 and 69, Appendix II). In defiance of the court-ordered closure of the Islamic Welfare Party, this same party resurrected itself under the new name of the Virtue Party (now *Fazilat Partisi*). The Virtue/Fazilat Party was the principal opposition to Prime Minister Bulent Ecevit, who had been instrumental in changing the constitutional Political Parties Law to prevent court action against this renamed Islamic party. Accommodating the pro-Islamic Virtue/Fazilat Party is one of those skillful political balancing acts which has worked favorably for Ecevit. He has managed to garner the opposition's support for the August 1999 constitutional amendments permitting foreign investment and privatization of state-owned industries (Wall Street Journal 8-16-99, A10).

When flexibility and accommodation go so far as to permit the election of officials from Islamic affiliated parties to office, usually the fundamental political agenda conflicts with secular structures. If the conflicts interfere with the planned path for continued internal national and external international alliances, the military has intervened and may continue to intervene, or pose a threat to redirect and protect the Atatürk legacy. Military intervention occurred in the 1960, 1971 and 1980 coups followed by the threat of military intervention in 1997. The later threat proved unnecessary when Erbakan, a member of an Islamic party, resigned in 1997.

The threat of military intervention seems to have decreased in direct proportion to the awareness of the consequences of political instability. Political instability decreases the capacity and effectiveness of the Turkish state; an ineffective state cannot conduct internal affairs and it cannot negotiate external international agreements. From the perspective of Keohane and Nye's complex interdependence (*Power and Interdependence*), Turkey is vulnerable and sensitive to the possibility of being perceived by more powerful stable nations passing judgment on its eligibility to join the EU and maintain membership in the OECD.

The balancing act that the Turkish government has employed in attempting to accommodate Islamic revitalization while maintaining the secular legacy of Turkey has tested its capability and effectiveness. By recommendation and monetary assistance, external organizations (OECD, its affiliates, IMF, World Bank, EU) have gradually impacted the internal political mechanisms of Turkish government. The OECD has assisted with economic advancement; the EU, IMF and the World Bank have assisted with both economic and political state capabilities for improved conditions in privatization of state industries and allocations for social security.

The IMF has been persuasive in influencing the Turkish parliament to permit international arbitration of disputes with foreign investors (public service projects); and to reduce the consultation time for contract negotiations with foreign partners and recognition of the privatization of state assets. Although privatization and foreign investment have remained low for Turkey, the economy has maintained an approximate annual growth rate of four and one tenths percent for the twenty-year period examined (OECD 1999, 111). The August 1999 parliamentary passage of recommended IMF amendments was achieved by Ecevit's skills in gaining the support of the opposition Virtue/Fazilat Party. Thus these accomplishments are a significant change in the 1982 constitutional provision for nationalization of industry and protection of state controlled public utilities (Wall Street Journal 8-16-99, A10). The passage of these IMF supported amendments, foreign investment and increased privatization, provide the opportunity for expansion in investments and assist Turkey to reach its goals. Expansion of the here-to-fore limited foreign investment and privatization set Turkey on its course for continued development and favorable review by the OECD, the EU and other organizations.

# World Bank's Role of the State

In 1997, the World Bank began focusing on state governments' capabilities to sustain achievements in political, economic and social developments. The rationale for renewed interest in the role of the state was based upon the simple timeless argument that political, economic and social development are impossible without a capable, effective state. The World Bank clarifies the distinction between a capable and an effective state as follows: a capable state has the ability to promote the rule of law and other infra-structures; an effective state uses its capability to further the interests and demands of society. Thus a state may be capable, but not effective, if its capability is not used to address the interests and demands of its citizens (World Bank 1997, 41-60).

Impetus for research and investigation into the state's role also came from the empirical evidence of the collapse of state command Communist governments and nations left stateless (Somalia and Liberia). An awareness of the polarized position of these stateless versus state-controlled nations persuaded the World Bank to establish criteria for stability and development beyond their former economic and technical concerns. Therefore, the 1997 study (World Bank 1997, 1-265) was concerned with the underlying structures that determine how economic and technical inputs are utilized by a capable and effective state. More specifically, does the state have the capacity to enforce the rule of law in facilitating and undergirding market transactions essential for effective sustainable development? This effective state the World Bank examined was found to be a partner, a facilitator rather than a director in market development. Market development and the role of the state is another area of difficulty confronting any nation's government if the fear of external control takes precedence over the possibilities for economic gains. In other words, the Turkish parliament has been reluctant to pass legislation for foreign investments. This fear of foreign investment and outside control was finally overcome with the August 1999 passage of legislation based on IMF recommendations. With parliamentary approval for foreign investment, it seems as if the Turkish state is acting as a facilitator for market development.

The World Bank does not claim that its reform concepts are guarantees for success. Rather they offer two basic guidelines: the state's activities must match its capabilities; and governments should concentrate on core factors crucial to development. Secondly, the principal question the World Bank addressed was: how can the government make the state's central institutions work better? After the World Bank examined sixty-nine countries, its research determined that markets and governments should work together. Certainly the state's government is necessary for establishing markets and institutions, but many states lack necessary foundations for market development. However, before considering market development, a state must demonstrate its capacity for a foundation of law; macroeconomic stability; social services and infrastructures; and the protection of the vulnerable members of society.

Assuming that the World Bank has established valid criteria for state/government stability and development, has Turkey demonstrated the capacity for these conditions? Regarding the first World Bank capacity, Turkey has transformed its legal system from Islamic law to the secular Swiss Civil Code—thereby facilitating international legal interaction. With respect to the second criterion, Turkey's macroeconomic stability, as reviewed by the OECD reports (1980-1999), indicates economic fluctuations, yet the consistent pursuit of economic advancement during this nineteen-year period. After the 60s, Turkey began a gradual progression from a less-developed to a developing state as substantiated by World Bank and OECD reports. The third capacity, social services and infrastructure, has been somewhat less successful than the preceding two. Although the constitution states that all Turkish citizens are entitled to social security (see constitution, part two, Articles 60 and 61, Appendix II), this entitlement is constrained by economic stability and more specifically, the sufficiency of financial resources. According to the 1999 OECD report, the quality and cost-effectiveness of the Turkish system of social assistance are inadequate. The share of Turkish social expenditures from the GDP is about seven percent as contrasted with twenty-five percent for OECD European countries. Reform measures suggested by the International Labor Office and reported by OECD include: an increase in the retirement age to sixty; an increase in insurable earnings; overall major improvements in the efficiency of social security institutions (based on stabilizing the public pay-as-you-go system); a secondary privately funded pension arrangement to assist in the development of financial markets; a system of social assistance for the disabled and elderly; and efforts to create a social consensus (OECD 1999, 92-110, and 148-149).

The fourth state capacity, protection of vulnerable societal members, relates to the previously discussed social security issues. Another difficult issue, the human rights of Kurds, repeatedly discussed by the EU, continues to plague the Turks, Kurds and EU members examining the problems of this unassimilated Kurdish population principally inhabiting the eastern provinces of Turkey and the contiguous borders with Iraq and Iran.

The twenty million Kurds are marginalized by their somewhat nomadic life and lack of integration into the mainstream of Turkish society. The international 1998-99 Ocalan incident (involving Italy, the Greek embassy in Africa and the EU), was used by the EU as a measuring guide to indicate Turkey's insufficient human rights record. As a result of Europe's reaction, Turkey postponed the previously pronounced death penalty against Ocalan, leader of the Kurdish Worker's Party. This decision was substantially confirmed by the high commissioner for foreign affairs and security, Javier Solana, who informed Prime Minister Ecevit that continued EU candidacy discussions are conditional. One of those conditions specifically states that Ocalan cannot be executed.

# The Kurdish Question

In an attempt to assimilate the Kurds in Turkey, Articles six and twenty-six of the constitution (see constitution, part one, Articles 6 and 26,

Appendix II) prohibit the exercise of sovereignty by an unauthorized source, or the use of another language, other than Turkish, by any outside group. This attempt at assimilation was viewed by Kurds and some Turkish scholars as suppressive. Several attempts were made to rescind the law related to Article twenty-six; however, it was not accomplished until the 1991 Gulf War focused attention on Iraq and Turkey. The creation of a Kurdish state in northern Iraq would encourage the Turkish Kurds who continue to request a separate state. In addressing this long-standing issue, President Ozal, in 1991, clearly stated that Turkey would not tolerate a separate Kurdish state in northern Iraq. The Iraqi Kurds were a serious issue for Turkey if they (the Iraqi Kurds) attempted to establish their own state. A Kurdish Iraqi state might make claims on Turkey's Kurdish eastern region, or aid the Turkish Worker's Party (PKK). If Turkey could influence the Iraqi Kurds to be pro-Turkish and act as their protector against the onslaughts of Saddam Husayn, it (Turkey) might win the respect of Europe. Winning the respect of Europe and alleviating concern for the human rights Kurdish question were important to the Turkish government, which has been and is interested in joining the European Union (Gunter 1992, 107).

Ozal, reflecting on the Kurdish problem and lack of past solutions, repealed the law prohibiting the use of the Kurdish language and granted amnesty to Turkish and Iraqi Kurds. Restrictions on the use of the Kurdish language were applied: it could be used for everyday conversation; it could not be used in official publishing, teaching or agencies. These concessions by the Turkish government prompted Ocalan to seek negotiations with Turkey. From 1984 to 1990, more than three thousand had been killed as a result of the PKK insurgency in Turkey. In November of 1991, Prime Minister Demirel made further concessions by declaring that Turkey should acknowledge "the Kurdish citizens' cultural identity must be recognized in full; that some citizens are not Turks but Kurds who belong to the Republic of Turkey" (Gunter 1992, 104).

The attempts of Ozal and Demirel seemed to fade when in March of 1992 a report from Sarnak accused the Turkish Workers Party of attacking townspeople. When it was discovered that defending security forces did not suffer casualties, a Helsinki Watch report confirmed that "the Turkish military and police forces were responsible for almost every casualty" (Helsinki Watch 1992, 14). Killings of Kurdish leaders continued by right-wing government hit squads referred to as

Hezbollah-contras (Gunter 1992, 106).[2] Finally, Ocalan accused Demirel of insufficient action; that his initiatives were merely words; that the Kurds must have their own national assembly, government and culture. Therefore, according to Ocalan's stance, violence on the part of the Kurdish people against the Demirel government would continue (Istanbul Milliyet 3-27-92, 42).

Intra-Kurdish hostilities between and among Turkish and Iraqi Kurds climaxed in the summer of 1992 when the PKK was responsible for the enactment of an embargo on trade between Turkey and northern Iraq. The effectiveness of the embargo caused the Iraqi Kurds to conduct assaults against the Turkish Kurds in an attempt to remove their presence from the triangle area of northern Iraq, Turkey and Iran. Turkish officials have accused Iraqi Kurds of assaults against the Turkish Kurds; and have charged that Saddam Husayn had been supplying the PKK with arms. Turkish officials also accused Husayn of cooperating with Ocalan as a retaliatory move against Turkey's cooperation with allied forces during the Gulf War. By the end of the Gulf War, the Kurds in each nation were divided as a result of foreign, Turkish and Arab governments' manipulation of the factional groups and parties (Kurds). Finally, allied and Turkish protection of the Iraqi Kurds in the north assisted in creating a de facto Kurdish government in Iraq (Gunter 1992, 112-113).

Fighting and terrorist activities between Turkish officials and Kurdish rebels, waged for fifteen years, continued after the Gulf War. The climax seemed to be reached when the PKK leader, Ocalan, with a price on his head, escaped to Europe. Turkey had charged him with treason and separatist movements against Turkey. These acts of treason were punishable by death (see constitution, part one, Articles 14 and 15, Appendix II) as determined by law. When Ocalan was finally captured in Nairobi by Turkish commandos in February of 1999, violent Kurdish attacks and killings occurred in Turkey, and demonstrations were staged throughout Europe (Berlin hosts over fifty thousand Kurdish workers). The international Ocalan affair captured headlines in major newspapers around the world; has been used by the EU human rights charter to indicate Turkey's inappropriate death sentence against Ocalan; and has been cited by the EU as a reason for the postponement of Turkey as a conditional membership candidate until December of 1999.

The Ocalan affair continues to be internally disruptive with regard to Turkish citizens harmed by PKK assaults. These citizens whose relatives have been assaulted by the PKK continue to clamor for the death sentence against Ocalan; and they denounce the political process for acquiescing to external pressure from the EU. This external pressure from the EU is a political litmus test for Turkey's acceptance of the European human rights charter. The internal affairs are focused on the families suffering the loss of Turkish officials who were killed by Kurdish uprisings. These families are clamoring for implementation of the death sentence to be carried out against Ocalan, and some called for the resignation of Ecevit, who has postponed the sentence. Externally, the EU has requested delay of Ocalan's death sentence until the human rights court reviews the case. After the court review, which could be prolonged as long as two years, the Turkish Parliament will receive the case. Meanwhile, Ecevit's balancing act between the internal and external political forces continued to test his seasoned political skills. These political skills used in balancing the internal with the externally related issues have become part of Turkey's globalization, interdependence and regionalization with other nations.

# Conclusion for Chapter 4

This research denies Huntington's arbitrary classification of Turkey as a "core Muslim state." The basis for the denial is based not only on Turkey's long-standing membership in the OECD, NATO, alliances with Israel, EU customs union and now EU candidacy, but it is also based upon Turkey's perception of itself, European recognition and the World Bank classification of Turkey as the "other Europe." Huntington's Islamic classification for the secular state of Turkey is an unfortunate example of insufficient knowledge about a state (in an effort to force a unit into his model).

This chapter focuses on the state capabilities identified by the World Bank as indicative of a state's ability to create and enact legislation beneficial to itself, its citizenry and its political, economic and social standing in the interdependent community of nation states. Despite three external global economic shifts influencing world markets and separate nation states; and despite internal political divisiveness, Turkey continues to meet the World Bank criteria for capability and effectiveness. The major areas identified by the World Bank in 1997 and met by

Turkey have been and continue to be: Turkey's transformed legal system; its relative macroeconomic stability; efforts to continue the development of its social services and infrastructures; and its ongoing efforts to meet EU membership criteria. The protection of Turkey's vulnerable societal members, as stipulated by World Bank criteria, continues to be questioned by the EU human rights division.

# Notes

1. According to Mehmet, the Islamic world needs a unifying institution. This can be achieved by recreating a modern version of the old Caliphate. . . . Turkey was the last trustee of this ancient office, and unilaterally took the decision to abolish it in 1924. This created a vacuum that has fragmented the world of Islam. Now Turkey has achieved a significant measure of development and self-confidence and has made major strides towards coming to terms with her rich Ottoman and Islamic past. It is a functioning democracy under the rule of law which must respect not only political dissent but also religious beliefs. These conditions did not exist in 1924, when the young Republic faced many dangers and threats, including those from regressive Islamic extremists scheming to abort Kemalist secularism (Mehmet 1990, 232-233).

2. On January 19th, 2000, Turkish police discovered ten bodies of kidnapped businessmen. The police suspect that the victims were kidnapped and killed by Hezbollah militants trying to form a separate Islamic state in the Kurdish sector of Turkey. The businessmen were apparently killed because they supported rival Islamic factions against the Hezbollah. According to authoritative sources, the Kurdish Hezbollah is not connected with the Lebanese Hezabollah. The Kurdish Hezbollah draws its support from poorly educated rural Kurds who have been responsible for random killings in Turkey. Foreign diplomats accuse Turkey's government of giving Hezbollah support and training in the 1980s in exchange for help in the fight against Abdullah Ocalan's Kurdistan Workers Party (PKK). Hezbollah has killed about sixty members of the PKK, but has never carried out an attack on police or other officials, focusing instead on attacking its rivals.

# Chapter 5

# Turkey in the OECD: 1980-1999

Turkey became a member of the Organization for Economic Cooperation and Development when it was established in 1961 for the purpose of achieving the highest sustainable economic growth and employment in each member nation and contributing to sound economic expansion and contributing to the expansion of world trade. Beginning in 1980, the OECD economic surveys reported the need for Turkey to develop an adequate export volume to not only assist it in offsetting the balance of payments deficits, but also to advance the internal economic structures. The introduction in 1980 of a stabilization and economic recovery program yielded results with a four percent increase in Turkey's GNP within a two year period (OECD 1983, 47).

This stabilization and economic restructuring process was assisted by market forces influencing resource allocation; the introduction of interest rates; devaluation and flotation of the Turkish monetary unit, the lira; and termination of state subsidized industries. These efforts, combined with a concerted effort to increase exports and reduce the budget deficit, decreased inflation and redressed the balance of payments (OECD 1985, 42). Redressing the balance of payments was a major achievement when Turkey was confronted with the external forces of high interest rates, protectionism in world trade markets and low commodity prices (OECD 1986, 40).

During the first six years (1980-1986), Turkey's economy progressed by approximately four and one-half percent each year under the OECD solidarity aid program of stabilization and structural adjustment (OECD 1987-1988, 91). Despite the gains Turkey made during most of the 1980s, weaknesses existed in the structure of exports.

Turkey's comparative advantage in the labor intensive production of textiles made this industry vulnerable to changes in world demand as well as protectionist measures enacted by other states. Continued trade reform in the areas of tariff reductions and the removal of import restrictions could reduce trade subsidies.

## State Economic Enterprises

One of the structural adjustment reforms beginning in 1980 targeted SEEs (State Economic Enterprises). Rather than reducing direct government intervention in price setting of goods, services and investments, the SEEs have remained under different government ministries. Additionally, since 1989 the decline in production and revenue of the SEEs has contributed to macroeconomic instability. The government has expressed its concern with reforms through privatization of the SEEs (OECD 1991-1992, 109).

The stagnation and macroeconomic deterioration Turkey experienced during 1990-1991 improved in 1993. The GNP expanded by an estimated seven percent, but was expected by OECD predictions to return to a sustainable five percent rate in 1994-1995. Responsibility for this growth and expansion was attributed to private investment, increased industrial capacity utilization, and easier access to consumer credit and household consumption. An important export factor for competitive trade prospects was the cooperative customs union arrangement between Turkey and the European Union in force by 1995. Before the customs union was in effect, continued reforms were necessary for improving Turkish trade and commercial laws. These laws had to express similarities and/or compatibility with those of the EU (OECD 1994, 93-98).

Structural reforms initiated in 1980 were identified in the 1990s as problems within the public sector. The public sector and the SEEs were classified as inefficient, too large, and thus a deficit to economic expansion. Therefore, targeted reform measures have included continued privatization of SEEs as well as budget constraints on those existing state economic enterprises classified as fiscal losses. These SEE reforms, recommended by the OECD, were necessary and expected as Turkey anticipated entry into the EU customs union in 1995. Markets in the EU customs union would demand reforms and compliance with standardized procedures if the Turkish economy were to adjust to the level of international competition. This lack of a competitive policy has been a factor preventing higher productivity within the SEEs and was predicted to be alleviated by entry into the customs union.

The advantages of membership in a customs union are competition, productivity and forming a consensus for facilitating structural reform coupled with constraints placed on macroeconomic policies (OECD 1995, 35-54). Thus in order to recognize benefits from the customs union, Turkey's responsibility rests with a continuation of speeding up the process of structural reforms and transforming its legal codes to be compatible and interact with legislation established within the EU. Considering that the EU is Turkey's largest export and import market for goods and services, it is in its (Turkey's) interest to fulfill the customs union EU agreement. In 1996, Turkey agreed to:

- eliminate all customs duties and quantitative restrictions on trade in industrial commodities with the EU;
- introduce the common EU customs tariff rates against third countries, but also adopt all preferential agreements the EU had made with third countries by 2001;
- ensure adequate and effective protection and enforcement of intellectual, industrial and commercial property rights;
- adopt the EU competition rules within a two year period (including measures regarding public aid). Structural adjustment aid would be granted for an additional five years (OECD 1996, 59).

Reforms of the SEEs and privatization have been slow as a result of the legacy of the 50s, 60s and 70s when import substitution and control planning managed to assist Turkey in establishing itself industrially in order to reach a middle income nation (one of the categories established by the World Bank to designate a nation's GDP). Economic reform measures in any nation may be on the drawing board and application examples from other successful states having implemented similar, effective measures, may be available. Yet the crucial issue of government acceptance and the willingness to implement reforms, may remain the obstacle for legislative approach of the proposed structural changes. Despite political interest groups' interference in the privatization process of the SEEs and the protracted time-frame for expediting the change from public to private ownership of state enterprises previously targeted, price-setting measures (for SEEs' products) could be accomplished. If SEEs are allowed to set prices and if the prices are competitive with international markets, exchange of goods is more easily facilitated. Price-setting in accordance with international markets also facilitates the sale or exchange of SEEs from public to private holdings. According to the 1997 OECD report:

> The aims of the Turkish program have not always been clear to the public. At times the government has sent out mixed signals about its intentions. Asset sales to reduce both public debt and subsidies to loss-making firms are a short-term goal. But the medium-term aims of such programs should be to receive "fair value" for government assets and to raise efficiency through greater competition and rational incentives structures. Thus, the sale of the loss-making Kardemir steelworks for one lira and writing off its debt, appears to have been an effective operation. Out-put doubled in 1996 and the workers accepted large real wage cuts. Hence, privatization created the conditions necessary to raise productivity and to cut costs, and the firm is now operating at a profit. By contrast, transferring a state monopoly to the private sector, without adequate regulatory controls, might raise government revenue, but do nothing to raise economic efficiency (OECD 1997, 69).

The textile industry provides an example of the tardy action by the Turkish government to prepare for reception into the EU customs union. As a customs union stipulation, competition legislation was passed in the Turkish parliament near the end of 1995. Establishing the competition boards remained a slow process to the extent that delays caused the EU to administer anti-dumping duties on textiles (OECD 1997, 61). After the EU administered the anti-dumping duties, Turkey began operating a Competition Authority in 1997 for the purpose of establishing regulations and rulings on competition infringements across the sectors of food, beverages, printing, publishing, cement, transportation and education. Independent, active Competition Authorities in other OECD member countries have been crucial in the promotion of general economic efficiency. Thus Turkey has within the past two years established procedures relating to potential conflicts between the regulations of certain agencies and legislation concerning competition (OECD 1999, 114).

When the state can not resolve conflicting interests among political actors and constituencies, these conflicts over the timing and methods of privatizing the SEEs and distributional issues are usually intensified. These conflicts occurred in Turkey after the 1995 election resulted in a lack of votes sufficient for any major political party to form a coalition government (even though several parties' political and economic platforms were similar).

Since 1980, the Turkish economy has averaged an annual growth rate of 4.1 percent. This growth rate has been possible as a result of three factors: extensive trade with its principal trading associate (the EU); a consistent growing work force (see Appendix IV); and a tradition of quality performance in private sector areas thus far established. Although Turkey's annual growth rate is higher than the OECD average of 2.5, the per capita Gross Domestic Product (GDP) remains the lowest among the OECD nations, equaling thirty percent of the OECD average (OECD 1999, 111-114).

After examining the status of the Turkish economy from information provided by the OECD surveys from 1980-1999, it is apparent that two areas in need of continual improvement are the SEEs and the political processes to enforce legislation suggested for improvements. Privatization of the SEEs has been in progress since 1984; however, state regulations remains significant in several industrial enterprises resulting from the reluctance of the government to release control. Thus the greatest structural challenge remains the passing of legislative reform policies and proposals through the political process.

OECD officials maintain that Turkey's bureaucrats prepare acceptable reform proposals, accompanied by sound policy advice. The continual difficulty seems to be getting these policies and proposals through the web of politics. The OECD council has recommended a plan to facilitate passage of proposed legislation. Its suggestion is a simple mandate for researching the costs and benefits of economic policies according to who wins and who loses from varying policy options. Research from costs and benefits would assist in strengthening policy procedures by identifying specific interests—the winners, losers and methods to overcome resistance to reform (OECD 1999, 119-134). Although establishing cost/benefit research analysis should identify the importance of effective government action in passing recommended legislation, the question of political stability (lack of military intervention) remains an equal, if not greater issue. Turkey's political stability, discussed as a separate issue in this book, has been an on-going problem regarding EU membership. According to the EU Commission,

Turkey exhibits basic features of a democratic system, yet it has failed to meet political membership requirements as a result of past military intervention, coups and weak coalitions. These conditions, viewed as characteristics of political instability, were reevaluated when Prime Minister Erbakan, in August of 1999, facilitated the passage of important legislation previously recommended by the OECD and the IMF. Within four months after this economic legislation was passed, the EU announced that Turkey was accepted as a conditional member.

# Turkey and the IMF

As a result of the 1960s-70s crises in the foreign exchange market, reforms initiated in the international monetary system allowed nations to select an exchange rate suitable for their economic objectives. The two choices were that a nation's currency could be determined by free markets floating rates or fixed against a standard of value. Member nations of the IMF,[1] in selecting one or the other choice, were required to conform to the following: rates can not be manipulated to interfere with balance of payments, nor can they gain an advantage over other IMF members; disorderly market conditions are prohibited; and all members' interests should be considered if any nation intervenes in exchange markets.

By 1992, out of one hundred fifty-four IMF members, seventy-six selected the fixed plan and seventy-eight selected managed or independent floating rates (Carbaugh 1995, 413). Turkey selected the managed floating plan in which exchange rates seem to reflect long-term economic forces underlying exchange rate movements of supply and demand. By following indicators (rates of inflation, foreign reserves and imbalances in international payments) that respond to similar economic forces as do exchange rates, Turkey can make necessary adjustments. Those necessary adjustments in the exchange rate can be made on the basis of the indicators for the international value of the lira. The currency exchange value of the Turkish lira (under flotation exchange rates) is determined by the market forces of supply and demand.

Although there are arguments for and against flotation exchange rates, any one nation does not strictly follow either the fixed or flotation method. The argument for the flotation system indicates that it is simple because continuous adjustments are somewhat automatic, resulting from supply and demand, and there seems to be a diminished need for international reserves. Demand for international reserves is based on the monetary value of international transactions and the amount and duration of balance-of-payments deficits.

The need for these reserves seems to be less necessary with the flotation exchange rates than it is under a fixed rate system (Carbaugh 1995, 480-81). Important for political and economic understanding are two tested principles: if international economic adjustment mechanisms are efficient and if international political policy coordination is extensive, the need for international reserves is limited. The arguments against floating include the possibilities for governments to pursue irresponsible financial policies and decisions accompanied by disorderly exchange markets and possible price inflation.

Turkey's option to pursue independent domestic policies (part of the flotation system), is partially held in check as a result of membership in the OECD, IMF and the EU customs union (compliance with managed organizational policies). As previously stated, nations do not necessarily follow either the fixed or flotation exchange rate. Turkey partially follows the fixed rate in that economic and political interdependence ties it to the rules and regulations of the IMF, OECD and the customs union. For example, the EU previously followed a system of joint floating in which currencies are linked by limitations on currency fluctuations (a range of 2.25 percent around the central exchange rate). This system was changed by the Maastricht Treaty of 1991 when member nations agreed to replace the European Monetary System (the 2.25 range) with the Euro single currency and a central bank. Turkey is held in check in terms of currency fluctuations, balance of payments deficits and stipulations from the EU regarding compliance with the customs union and other issues before full membership can be considered.

# Balance of Payments

As indicated in Table One (page 55), from 1980-1999 Turkey has experienced a balance of payments (BOP) deficit (the difference between the export/import figures). The exchange rate adjustments previously discussed, influence a nation's balance of payments and secondarily influence domestic economy (Carbaugh 1995, 453). At the recommendation of the OECD, Turkey has periodically devalued the lira to partially resolve the BOP deficits as well as receiving IMF loans for this purpose. Pursuing a policy of devaluation or revaluation is dependent upon other nations refraining from attempts to offset exchange-rate adjustments implemented by the country with the deficits. Thus economic interdependence among nations requires cooperation of one nation with the other.

## Neo-classical Economic Influence

The 1980s ushered in the measurable influence neo-classical economists produced on the issue of international development. The neo-classical economists shifted from the Keynesian approach concerned with "getting the policies right to getting the prices right." The IMF and the World Bank accepted and utilized neo-classical recommendations based upon a combination of strategies:

1.  The public sector should be reduced
2.  Foreign trade should be liberalized; the incentive for inward-looking economic behavior should be replaced by outward export economic activity
3.  Distorting interventions (the state, actors, others) in the pricing mechanisms should be eliminated in order to achieve maximum growth and development (Martinussen 1997, 257-264)

Regarding the application of these three strategies, the OECD reports on Turkey since 1980 have consistently recommended privatization of public sectors. The OECD has also been influential in recommending export-oriented growth. That recommendation has provided a rationale for EU customs union non-tariff advantage on imports and exports. Turkey has attempted to pursue trade liberalization policies through diminished state intervention in the pricing of goods as previously noted in the textile industries. External constraints imposed by the OECD and the EU customs union have been instrumental in pricing issues.

These trade liberalization policies were incorporated into World Bank recommendations for structural adjustment loans to Turkey beginning in the 1980s. These loans have been criticized from various perspectives, especially those advocating policy reforms accompanied by methods to stabilize the Turkish economy. Although Aricanli and

Rodrik have criticized the 1980-1984 World Bank structural adjustment loans to Turkey, they have also acknowledged some benefits. Their chief criticism focuses on the bank's prescriptions for economic liberalization without incorporating a mechanism for economic stability and thereby guaranteeing Turkey's ability to sustain and monitor progress and growth as it occurred and may continue to occur. As far as the benefits are concerned, Turkey received $1,080.3 million dollars from the World Bank from 1980-1984 (Aricanli and Rodrik in Thomas 1991, 458-459). As a result of these loans, Turkey avoided the usual procedure of controlling economic growth during the time when adjustments must be identified, monitored and compared, and mechanisms established for examining what constitutes successful structural changes for sustainable economic growth (procedures for adjustments were part of the loan conditions). Turkey also benefited because its government policies were prepared to receive a structural adjustment World Bank loan.

This World Bank loan was introduced to Turkey on the basis of the bank's conditions and adherence to the policy of trade liberalization. Liberalization of trade occurs when there is minimal, yet sufficient government intervention to help reform a country's international, commercial policies in order to improve economic stability. In turn, economic stability is actualized when government regulations are relaxed and reliance on changes in the pricing system can be realized. The World Bank loan was offered at the time when Turkey was under military rule from 1980-1983. Because the loan was supported during the time of trade liberalization, when government/state intervention was at a minimum, the temporary military leadership accepted the terms of the loan without the usual political negotiations between the government/state and the loan officials. However, with the return to parliamentary democracy in November of 1983, restrictions on trade were imposed. The return to elections and a multi-party system affected the extension of economic liberalization in a way that increased the state's discretionary power and control over the economic resources of Turkey (Aricanli and Rodrick in Thomas 1991, 32). With the termination of the loans in 1984, the capacity for the Turkish government to establish mechanisms for economic sustainability were limited at a time when the government had been in crisis.

Table 1 indicates that from 1980-1984, the balance of payments was decreasing and exports and imports were increasing. However,

## TABLE 1

**Exports, Imports and Balance of Payments
for Turkey from 1980-1998**
(in US dollar equivalency-million $)
*Figures are compiled from separate, yearly OECD publications*

| Year | Exports | Imports | Balance of Payments |
|------|---------|---------|---------------------|
| 1980 | 2910 | 7513 | -4603 |
| 1981 | 4703 | 8567 | -3864 |
| 1982 | 5890 | 8518 | -2628 |
| 1983 | 5905 | 8895 | -2990 |
| 1984 | 7389 | 10331 | -2942 |
| 1985 | 8255 | 11230 | -2975 |
| 1986 | 7583 | 10664 | -3081 |
| 1987 | 10322 | 13551 | -3229 |
| 1988 | 11929 | 13706 | -1777 |
| 1989 | 11780 | 15999 | -4219 |
| 1990 | 13026 | 22581 | -9555 |
| 1991 | 13672 | 21007 | -7340 |
| 1992 | 14892 | 23082 | -8190 |
| 1993 | 15610 | 29772 | -14162 |
| 1994 | 18390 | 22606 | -4216 |
| 1995 | 21975 | 35187 | -13212 |
| 1996 | 32446 | 43028 | -10582 |
| 1997 | 32647 | 48005 | -15358 |
| 1998 | 31128 | 45540 | -14412 |

with a military government in temporary power for most of this time frame, and a liberalized economy supported by the loan, insufficient attention was given to either economic or political stability. With the major reorganization of government administration, beginning in 1983, the new program focused on exposing the economy to market forces and international competition. This effort supported conditions for medium-term growth (additional support for placing Turkey in the middle-income states). The period from 1980-1984 was politically and economically critical for Turkey and raises questions for examination. Were the mechanisms for economic stabilization overlooked because of the 1980 government crisis and the subsequent military intervention until 1983? Did the World Bank issue the $1,080.3 million loan over a four year period because of Turkey's government crisis and social disruption? Were the loans a result of the bank's interest in assisting Turkey in the process of structural adjustments and eventually stabilization? Even if the answer to all three questions is yes, the researcher is still confronted with the critical issue of determining whether or not external agencies (World Bank and others) are indirect causes of political and economic disruption and instability. To address this issue of endogenous factors as direct or indirect causes of instability, it is necessary to review the theoretical economic shifts with which nations were expected to comply in their pursuit of increased, measurable growth.

If a nation's economic, political and social structures are not working cooperatively, or are not at compatible developmental levels, then the state experiences internal unrest resulting from both endogenous and exogenous pressures. The compatible development levels are predicated on the assumption that the government structure has the stability and capacity to recognize, authorize, and accept perceived necessary economic and social reforms. Exogenous and endogenous political and social disruption and economic policy shifts have plagued Turkey in its pursuit of reforms. Emphasis in this section of the book is focused on economic reforms since 1980 and political and social issues are addressed in chapter three.

Prior to 1980, economists referred to the period before 1973 as dominated by Keynesian economic theory. These classical economists were aware that the purchasing power of a surplus nation rose relative to that of a deficit nation with an impact on imports in each nation. The Keynesian theory suggested that the influence of purchasing power changes in surplus and deficit nations automatically helped restore payments to equilibrium. If payment imbalances are persistent, a surplus nation will experience rising income and imports will increase. Conversely, a deficit nation will experience a fall in income and a decline in imports (Carbaugh 1995, 384).

Neo-classical economists were dissatisfied with this seemingly fixed, intractable system of government intervention, control and getting the "policies right." Thus neo-classical economists began focusing on trade liberalization and getting the "prices right." Privatization of the SEEs and economic liberalization of trade from the 1980s to the 90s were exogenous recommendations for Turkey by the World Bank and OECD as well as the push to develop export markets to offset the balance of payments deficits.

Turkey was once again confronted with yet another economic policy shift based upon the magnitude and influence of the OECD and World Bank recommendations. If loan grants were to be conditional and based upon acceptance of trade liberalization and implementation of external regulations, should Turkey comply? These liberalized policies meant that Turkey's public SEEs were to be deregulated; that they were to be privatized. Thus Turkey, anxious to receive assistance and continue its development policies with aspirations for acceptance into the EU, complied with the shift and embarked on liberalized, economic policies that created political disruption and societal unrest.

## The Third Economic Shift of the 1990s

With respect to the restructuring of the Turkish economy, neo-classical liberalized economic theory had dominated the decade of the 1980s to the 1990s. The IMF and the World Bank were among those institutions accepting the recommendations of neo-classical economists. These institutions utilized the recommendations as conditions for their structural adjustment loans to Turkey. These conditions granted the World Bank an opportunity to influence the economic policy of nations receiving their loans (Martinussen 1997, 263).

Prior to the 1980s, the state-managed development model had prevailed and was adaptable to Turkey's SEEs and successive five-year economic plans. Then the 1980s ushered in neo-classical, liberalized economic policies with conditional loans. These loans were granted on the condition that Turkey would implement, adjust and change the state-managed economic policies. Thus Turkey, well before the 1980s had been confronted with exogenous conditional economic policies which affected the stability of their endogenous political policies.

Near the end of the 1980s, a somewhat modified approach emerged which seemed to incorporate the former state managed plan with that of the liberalized market-led model beginning in 1980. Another economic shift was on the drawing board advocating the need for capacity-building within state structures. The World Bank through its discussion of the distribution of labor between the state and markets, shifted from its support for a liberalized economic approach to what seemed a middle ground position (World Bank, 1997, 41-61). The theory behind the middle ground third shift of the 1990s reflected the appropriate division of labor between the state and the markets by trying to avoid failures in either one (the state or the markets). The seemingly important part of this economic theory is based upon the way in which the state acts as well as the relationships established with the private sector. Therefore, government interventionism should determine which organizations should be privatized, commercialized or unchanged. Thus the key question is centered on what is politically and economically feasible at the specific time when changes are anticipated.

Concerning economic and political feasibility, the task is to establish workable conditions between the private sectors and the state. In support of this position, the World Bank economists advocated a non-interventionist approach in cases where markets seem to work efficiently and productively. Conversely, states should judiciously intervene in cases where markets are unreliable, unproductive and inefficient. These feasibilities are predicated upon the assumptions that political support for policy reforms can and should be solicited (Martinussen 1997, 266). The World Bank, influential in assisting with Turkey's structural reforms, began the 80s advocating neo-classical, liberalized economic policies, but began a new decade, the 90s, emphasizing the necessity for state structure capacity-building and case by case governmental intervention. Thus at the beginning of the 90s, the focus was on the feasible distribution of labor between the state and markets.

# Conclusion for Chapter 5

Although Turkey has improved its economic standing by gradually implementing OECD recommendations during the 1980-1999 period, infrastructure and SEE reforms are incomplete. The SEEs remain a difficult segment of the economy consistently targeted by the OECD. These state-owned enterprises were constructed under the aegis of etatism (state industrial control similar to command economies). Turkey's economists could understand and cope with that sector of Keynesian economic theory advocating state intervention; however, accommodating neo-classical economic policies would be disruptive; it would require restructuring of state-controlled enterprises. Neo-classical economic theory, commonly known as economic liberalization, was endorsed and recommended by the OECD and World Bank for all member nations. Thus Turkey, comfortable with its government-controlled enterprises, was confronted with exogenous recommendations for economic policy changes that the government seemingly supported, yet could not legislate during periods of unstable government.

The lack of government capacity to approve and legislate privatization of the SEEs occurred during difficult periods of Turkey's political development as a relatively new republic. The post 1980 military coup entailed a time of recovery; the periods from 1991-1996 were marked by weak coalition governments; and exogenous international liberalized markets could not be ignored, or Turkey might fall prey to the plight of a less-developed nation. Government capability to pass important economic legislation endorsed by the World Bank, International Monetary Fund, and the OECD was in the procedural stages during the administration of Prime Minister Ecevit and President Demirel. These two seasoned politicians shared similar ideals for the economic development of Turkey and its reliance upon external economic organizations.

The 1990s economic shift supported and recommended by the World Bank, entailed examination of criteria determining a state's capacity to govern, to adopt legislation and to effectively administer those adopted policies. The basic economic concept examined and supported by the World Bank focused on a nation's markets, industries and enterprises. If they had been profitable and well-regulated, then government intervention was not necessary. Conversely, those markets, industries and enterprises deemed unprofitable should be examined by the government. This economic shift seemed reasonably compatible with Turkey's understanding of government intervention; however, the problem focused on those unprofitable SEEs still regulated by the state, yet repeatedly recommended for privatization. As late as 1998, planned privatization of twenty-six companies had been delayed until 1999; and they remain under examination (OECD 1999, 119). The OECD remains forceful in its recommendations for continued privatization of those state industries operating at losses with wages exceeding sales revenue. The OECD nineteen volumes were published before the administration of Demirel and Ecevit began passing recommended legislation in August of 1999. Therefore, effective policies for increased privatization were receiving attention. Now it is the responsibility of the new administration under Prime Minister Recep Erdoğan to continue these privatization policies.

# Note

1. The International Monetary Fund (IMF) was one of two international institutions established near the end of World War II to ease the transition from a wartime to a peacetime environment and to help prevent a recurrence of the turbulent economic conditions of the Great Depression era. The IMF and the World Bank were established at the United Nations Monetary and Financial Conference held at Breton Woods, New Hampshire in July of 1944. The World Bank's main purpose is to make long-term development and reconstruction loans, whereas the IMF provides short-term balance-of-payments adjustment loans. The IMF includes more than 150 nations. The goals of the IMF are: to promote international cooperation by providing the means for members to consult on international monetary issues, to facilitate the growth of international trade and foster a multilateral system of international payments; to promote stability of exchange rates and seek the elimination of exchange restrictions that disrupt international trade; and to make shorterm financial resources available to member nations on a temporary basis as to allow them to correct payments disequilibria without resorting to measures that would destroy national prosperity. . . . All IMF loans are subject to some degree of conditionality. This means that to obtain a loan, a deficit nation must agree to implement economic and financial policies as stipulated by the IMF. These policies are intended to correct the member's balance-of-payments deficit and promote noninflationary economic growth (Carbaugh 1995, 462).

# Chapter 6

## The European Union and Turkey

This chapter examines the rationale for Turkey's entry into the EU. The rationale began with the conceptualization that the customs union agreement of 1995 with the well-established EU economic organization (in cooperation with the OECD), continues to be a major contributing factor to improving Turkey's export/import markets and balance of payments (as indicated in Table One of the preceding chapter). During the short passage of time (including the beginning stages of conceptualizing the research design), not only has Turkey experienced a political change; Turkey was granted membership candidacy status in December of 1999. As discussed in Chapter Three, the parliamentary election of Prime Minister Ecevit seemingly sent a message to the EU Commission that a stable, European-oriented government was in power. Ecevit was not only an experienced politician untainted by scandal; he was also a respected former government official who satisfied the mass populace and the watch-dog military. This latter point, in recent years, has been a difficult achievement. It has been difficult because the revitalization of Islam has fueled the continuation of Islamic parties with political agendas dissimilar to those of secular parties. Those differing agendas had created unresolved conflicts necessitating intervention by the military, persistent in its intent upon maintaining a secular government. Although Islamic political parties had been constitutionally prohibited, subsequent laws approved by Prime Minister Ecevit and President Demirel were passed protecting Islamic parties. As a result, the Ecevit administration diplomatically recognized the status of Islamic parties; and sought their cooperation in support of recent legislation dealing with foreign investment; continuation of privatization of government-held enterprises; and agreements with the EU commission regarding conditions that must be met before Turkey's membership can be completed. These two changes, one internal (the election of Prime Minister Ecevit), and the other external (EU membership candidacy status), are empirical evidence supporting the thesis that Turkey has demonstrated political stability from 1998 to 2007; and that economically, it is a middle-income nation state. Since 1999, internal political stability has enabled Turkey to improve its standing with an external economic organization, the EU. The regulations required by the EU will also legitimize and expand the "suitcase trade" transacted between Turkey and Central Asia because Turkey has a customs union with the EU which permits trade restrictions on non-member states. Unlike a free trade area which would allow Turkey to set its own standards for trade with Central Asia, the customs union status with the EU specifies restrictions on nonmembers which could expand, yet regulate the "suitcase trade," or remain at its current unregulated status.

Not only does improvement in exports and imports (in compliance with EU specifications), assist Turkey and the members of the EU core nations, but liberalized, standardized markets expand trade with other nations. While trade with other middle-income and/or core nations is important, trade with the less developed nations (marginalized by specialized, globalized markets), contributes to the democratization of the inequitable capitalist markets. Thus, less developed nations marginalized by specialized, globalized markets, are afforded the opportunity to trade with middle-income nations whose products are more reasonably priced than those from the core nations. Some of these products purchased by Central Asia from Turkey are non-tariff as a result of EU competition and other agreements.

## The EU Structure

The EU, created as the EC in 1957 by the Treaty of Rome, established the following provisions:

1. elimination of tariffs, quotas and trade restrictions for member states
2. tariffs charged on commodities from non-member states
3. free movement of capital, labor and enterprise for member states

4.  common transport of agricultural products and competitive policies
5.  the coordination of member state's monetary and fiscal policies.

Economic integration for the EU members has achieved liberalized trade payments and factor input mobility. Integration continues to be accomplished through the developmental stages of free trade areas, customs union, common markets, an economic union, and a monetary union. Integration within the EU membership continues to be possible as a result of institutions created to meet political challenges and the complexities of economic growth. These EU institutions, because they have representatives from each of the member states, are intrinsically democratic and flexible in terms of their decision making procedures. These institutions consist of the following legislative, executive and judicial bodies:

the Parliament – a legislative body with control over the use of executive power

the Council – a supranational and intergovernmental organization

the Commission – the center of the EU's policy-making process

the Court of Justice – a uniform body of rules expressed as community law

the Court of Auditors – a financial conscience—a guarantor of administrative and accounting principles

the Investment Bank – a cost-effective source of finance—the largest financing institution in the world

the Economic and Social Committee – a representative of the different sectors of civil society

the Committee of the Regions – a new body for regional issues

the Ombudsman – acts as a conciliator between citizens and EU institutions.[1]

# A Customs Union

Empirical evidence indicates that the EU has benefited from trade creation that has out-weighed losses from trade diversion. The point is that free trade in a customs union affects global trade in two opposing ways:

a welfare-increasing trade-creation effect and a welfare-reducing trade-diversion effect. The trade-creation effect consists of consumption and production effects. Trade creation, through a customs union is designed to add to global welfare. Conversely, trade diversion creates a welfare loss because it (trade diversion) happens when imports from a low-cost supplier, external to the union, are replaced by purchases from a higher-cost supplier in the customs union. Thus the question is: what nation states benefit from a customs union? If nations had a competitive economy before joining a customs union, they will benefit from trade creation through the opportunity to increase competitiveness (Carbaugh 1995, 246-270).

Economic integration in the EU fosters competitiveness, economies of scale and investment spending. In order for a customs union to yield welfare gains, the consumption and production benefits of trade-creation should outweigh the losses from trade-diversion. The term welfare is used to describe the benefits to societal members of those states belonging to an integrated economic organization. The term welfare also refers to the well-being of those societal members. The problem is that this level of well-being may fluctuate according to the degree of economic integration of any organization. For example, the EU has evolved from free trade areas, a customs union, and a common market, to the final stage of integration, the economic union. In this final stage of economic integration, special EU institutions act as administrators to establish agreements for national social taxation and fiscal policies.

Turkey's current status and identity with the EU is at the level of a customs union, one degree of advancement beyond the free trade areas. In other words, now that Turkey has been accepted as a conditional member, there are two stages of advancement beyond the customs union which current members have achieved, or are in the process of achieving. With the customs union agreement, Turkey freely trades with its first trading partners, EU members, on the basis of nontariffs on products for export/import. The EU offers member nations the possibility for increased competition and product specialization (see OECD Chapter 5). Studies have indicated that the greater the number of nation states in a union, the greater the gain will be as a result of the possibility that low-cost producers will be regional members. The scope for trade diversion is less when the customs union's external tariff is lower. A lower tariff permits increased trade with non-member nations. Therefore, less replacement of cheaper imports from non-member nations by high-cost imports will occur (Carbaugh 1995, 248-250).

Before Turkey was granted customs union status in 1995, it had satisfied some of the criteria necessary for welfare enhancement. It has been estimated that the welfare gain for Turkey will be in the one to one and five-tenths percent of the GDP per year, with large gains from increased access to less developed markets. (This projected information supports this research concept that Turkey is in the process of alleviating the inequalities in the less-developed nations.) In 1994, Turkey's exports to the EU were forty-seven percent and imports were forty-six percent. Then in 1997, Turkey's exports to the EU were about forty-six percent and imports were fifty-one percent (Hartler & Laird 1999, 4). This percentage change may indicate a slight decrease in exports from Turkey to the EU (with some to the less-developed nations), while imports from the EU to Turkey began a slight increase in 1997 (see Appendix V).

Since Turkey was granted access to an EU customs union as late as 1995, trade creation was not immediately within its grasp, because time was needed to develop specialization of products. This specialization develops as members of the EU determine diversification of products that are available within the EU regional organization. Subsequent to product diversification, decisions are made about the commodities each member nation will select for specialization. This specialization process, as previously discussed, increases the dependence of each nation upon the others. Therefore, the overall interdependence among not only the EU members, but in the globalized market, is directly proportional to the degree of product specialization pursued by each nation. In addition to specialization, competitiveness of products is another issue in the process of trade creation. In 1997 Turkey established an independent Competition Authority based on EU competition law comprised of agreements, practices in restraint of competition, abuse of dominant position and mergers and acquisitions affecting Turkey's markets. According to article thirty-four of the customs union, any aid which distorts or threatens competition by favoring production of certain goods will be (if it affects trade between the EU and Turkey), incompatible with the functioning of the customs union. Aid to promote economic development of Turkey's less developed regions is supposedly allowed until January of the year 2001.

After 1970, the EU had achieved a customs union status for all members; however, by 1985, concern was focused on the competitive capacity of the organization. To meet the challenge of global competitiveness, the EU issued a plan for the development of the common market in its progress toward economic integration. These plans called for the removal of barriers to border controls, standards, regulations, business laws and protectionist government policies. By removing these barriers to the transactions occurring between and among the EU states, a possible market of about three hundred and twenty-five million customers could be realized. EU officials estimated that their intra-state market economy would be second only to the US. The effects of a complete common market would probably create an immediate supply-side shock which in turn would lead to cost decreases. Therefore, prices would fall as a result of pressure from competitors from formerly protected markets. Price decreases usually create an increase in demand. This increase in demand permitted firms and companies to expand their output, efficiently use their resources and in general prepare for EU member and global competition (Carbaugh 1995, 250-259).

An expanded EU market would allow firms to produce according to economies of scale (reduced minimum average costs resulting from the increased size/scale of firms and equipment); decrease unit costs (hourly wage rate divided by output per labor-hour) and increase product output. Economies of scale are usually industries with less, yet larger firms standardized by product output, and are usually limited to the industries listed below.

| | |
|---|---|
| motor vehicles | electrical engineering |
| other transportation | instrument engineering |
| chemicals | paper and publishing |
| fibers | mineral products |
| metals | rubber and plastics |
| office machinery | drink and tobacco |
| mechanical engineering | food (Gowland & James 1991, 27) |

From the above list of importable and or exportable goods, Turkey excels in articles of iron and steel, food products and tobacco. In these products, Turkey's exports exceed imports (see Appendix V).

The 1991 Maastricht Summit produced plans for an economic and monetary union (EMU) and the European Political Union (EPU). Achievement of the EMU called for free movement of capital; coordination of monetary policies; establishment of a Euro Monetary Institution for coordinating monetary policies; and the establishment of a European Central Bank for the common currency.[2] Regarding the EPU, member nations agreed upon defense and foreign policies compatible with NATO. Also, the EPU made provisions for a common visa policy and an EU citizenship permitting citizens to vote in elections outside their own states.

In addition to industrial provisions, the EU established a common agriculture policy (CAP) which replaced the separate member state stabilization policies. CAP supports prices for farmer's products. The EU employs export subsidies to guarantee that surplus agricultural output can be sold outside the member states. The CAP high price supports have enabled farmers to increase production. The EU pays the farmers export subsidies in order for them to sell surplus quantities outside member states at a lower price, yet receive higher support prices (Carbaugh 1995, 255). Turkey excels in agricultural products with a higher export to import ratio. Therefore Turkey will benefit from the subsidies and the CAP high price supports.

The EU has liberalized government procurement policies by allowing all members to bid for any government public contracts. Government purchases in the EU account for around fifteen percent of the total GDP. Government purchases usually consist of transportation equipment, telecommunications, business services, energy products and building/civil engineering. Therefore, in order for the EU to become a complete common market, former restrictions related to government purchases and their suppliers were liberalized. This liberalized policy opened a large market to all EU states. It enabled any member to submit a bidding contract as a possible supplier to the government of any other member. Criteria for contract awards hinges on the lowest price, but includes product quality, reliability and delivery dates (Carbaugh 1995, 257). If Turkey has not completed the privatization of its SEEs by the time of acceptance to full membership, this liberalized contracting arrangement may be beneficial.

# Candidacy Status

The current stage of development in EU-Turkish negotiations provides Turkey with a customs union and the recent candidacy status for future full membership into the union. At the December 11, 1999 Helsinki conference, EU leaders welcomed Turkey as a candidate on the basis of compliance with prescribed recommendations. The Helsinki conference ended with the resolution that candidacy discussions can not begin until Turkey improves its human rights record and settles disputes with Greece. After the Helsinki conference, Turkey has initiated activity in compliance with the EU requests in the two required areas. First the sentence of the Kurdish KPP leader, Ocalan, was delayed and subject to EU review. Secondly, the Turkish and Greek foreign ministers met on January 20, 2000 to sign peace pledge accords. These accords include: the regulation of commerce, protection of investments (investors not subject to double taxation), prevention of illegal immigration, promotion of tourism, and protection of the Aegean area. The signing of these accords was facilitated by the cordial meetings between the Greek Foreign Minister Papandreau and former Turkish Prime Minister Ecevit. Turkey's incentives for these accords range from an interest in compliance with EU requests to the reduction of barriers between Greece and Turkey. Logically the EU does not want two states in disharmony as members of the union (Greece, a current member and Turkey, a candidate for membership). After Greece relinquished its veto power for Turkey's EU candidacy, EU membership was extended on a conditional clause in the draft. The membership draft stated that the EU, through the International Court of Justice, would review any territorial disputes and "promote their settlement." The draft was discussed by Solana, the EU's Commissioner for Foreign Affairs, with former Prime Minister Ecevit. The membership draft indicated that Turkey and Greece were granted a five-year period in which to resolve the 1974 hostile division of Cyprus into the Greek and Turkish sectors.

The signing of the Greek/Turkish accords was facilitated by the resignation of the foreign minister of Greece who was replaced by Papandreou. The former Greek foreign minister and his intelligence officers were caught in a scandal involving the protection of the Kurdish leader, Ocalan. This Kurdish leader had been illegally, yet successfully protected by Greece's former foreign minister from the time of his flight to Europe until his capture in Kenya.

The Finland EU president was unable to resolve the Cyprus dispute. This dispute involves the Greek part of Cyprus, the Republic of Cyprus, and the Turkish sector under Turkey's control. This legal and governmental division has resulted in a decision by the Greek Cypriot government to not open trade with Northern Cyprus, and Turkey has refused to open its transportation accesses to the Republic of Cyprus, despite the terms of the Ankara Protocol, calling for opening of the ports, airports and roads. Lack of a resolution to this dispute continues to be an impediment to Turkey's accession to the EU.

## Economic Criteria for EU Membership

The EU commission's decision to accept Turkey as a candidate for membership was based upon factors other than Greek/Turkish relations and the Kurdish issues. The commission regularly examines the OECD's published reports on economic developments in Turkey. The review process has included the progress of Turkey before 1980; however, the past twenty years have passed without military intervention, and the recent five-year period marks the accession of Turkey's acceptance into the customs union and conditional membership. The EU has examined the OECD's reports on Turkey's fiscal policy to determine economic criteria for membership. Basic economic policy objectives important for international transactions between and among nations are referred to as the balance of payments structure in each state. The two fundamental BOP transactions are current and capital accounts. The current account is the monetary value of the flow of goods, services and unilateral transfers (goods and services are exports or imports). Goods and services Turkey exports are considered credits to the BOP system; goods and services Turkey imports are considered as debits to the BOP system. If Turkey's current account indicates that imports exceed exports, then its balance of payments reflects a deficit. Conversely, if the current account indicates an excess of exports, then there is a surplus. The exports and imports determine a nation's GDP status: a plus balance on the current account indicates that exports are in excess over imports and the difference is added to the GDP; a minus indicates that imports are in excess over exports and are subtracted from the GDP. If the exports of goods and services are equal to the imports, then a nation's GDP status would be unaffected by either additions or subtractions. Unilateral transfers, part of a nation's current account system, are one-way transactions of goods or services. In other words, the goods or services may be gifts or foreign aid for which there is no remittance (one-way transactions).

The capital account, the other balance of payments transaction, is purchases or sales of assets. These assets are real estate titles, stocks, bonds, government securities and commercial bank deposits. Capital accounts may be direct investments (for example: an EU member with controlling interest in a Turkish business); securities (purchases of debt security of private enterprise, SEEs); and bank claims and liabilities (loans and demand deposits). The capital account transactions are recorded with a plus credit to capital coming into Turkey and a minus debit to capital outflows from Turkey. Thus capital inflow means that Turkey is receiving payment for its exports; capital outflow means that Turkey is paying money for its imports. When Turkey experiences a current account deficit, its expenditures for imports are greater than the income from its exports. Thus Turkey must finance its current account deficit. Financing the deficit can be accomplished by selling assets and/or borrowing. Therefore when Turkey experiences a current account deficit, it is financed by an inflow of capital into the capital account by borrowing or from external loans.

The factors persuading Turkey to change economic policies were the BOP problems, the failed attempts of trade liberalization during the 1970s, high inflation, unemployment problems and substantial foreign borrowing. The liberalization policies beginning in 1980 were initially focused on restructuring the economy from etatism to a market economy, alleviating the BOP problem and expanding exports. Prior to 1980 Turkey primarily exported agricultural products and imported industrial products. The imbalance between incoming revenue from agrarian products versus the outgoing expenditures for imports continued to create the BOP deficits. By focusing on measures to correct this deficit, manufactured products increased from a twenty-nine percent share in 1980 to a sixty-nine percent share in 1991 (Pomfret 1991, 76-88). From the share of exportable commodities, textiles exceeded other exports with fifteen percent in 1980 and thirty-two percent in 1991. The remainder of the exports beginning with 1980 included: hides, leather, iron, steel, rubber, non-ferrous metals, chemicals, ceramics, bricks and tiles.

From the foregoing exports, iron, steel, rubber and ceramics are economies of scale which provide for larger output and greater product variety. It is assumed that economies of scale create increases and gains in trade. However, the problem of economies of scale for Turkey hinges on the fact that its principal trading associates are highly industrialized nations with higher levels of capital accumulation and production technology. Thus Turkey at the outset of 1980 emerged from inter-industry trade (the exchange between nations of differentiated industrial products) to intra-industry trade (two-way trade in a similar product). Although specialization of products occurs in both inter-industries and intra-industries, after World War II industrialized countries have focused on what might be referred to as sub-specialization. In other words, rather than focusing on specialization within a complete industry (inter-industry), highly industrialized nations have directed their efforts to the specialization of some aspect of a pre-existing specialized industry (intra-industry). For example, two or more nations may conduct trade in the same product. The problem is that the EU nations began intra-industry trade around 1945, whereas Turkey began as late as 1980 with two-way trade. This two-way intra-industry trade between the highly developed EU/OECD nations and the developing nation of Turkey clearly demonstrates a differentiation in quality. There is a difference in the production factors resulting from capital-intensive technology versus labor-intensive production. The accumulated capital of the EU nations will be used for capital-intensive technology production, whereas Turkey will utilize labor-intensive production resulting from a lack of accumulated capital. The Turkish government had focused on exportable manufactured goods; however, labor-intensive products accounted for about thirty-seven percent of the exports in the 1990s and capital accumulation lagged (OECD 1980-1992 & Taskin and Yeldan, 1996, 155). The measures to correct the deficits were a flexible exchange rate policy, promotion of manufactured exports and gradual liberalization of imports. Trade liberalization assisted Turkey as a result of the elimination or reduction of protectionist tariffs and quotas, a change in policy from import-substitution to manufactured exports, and the capacity to receive imports without creating substantial deficits (Baysan and Blitzer 1991, 263).

The foregoing discussion regarding the balance of payments (BOP) is important because it represents Turkey's external balance status (refer to Table One in Chapter 5). The external balance represents Turkey's situation with regard to limited deficits or a surplus in imports and exports. In other words, when the EU examined Turkey's status for membership, the external balance of Turkey's current account should not reflect a foreign debt that it could not repay. Conversely, Turkey should not reflect a surplus that could not be repaid by other nations. This latter situation has not occurred in terms of Turkey's international trade with EU members. However, as Turkey increases its trade with Central Asia, the potential for a surplus could occur (the plus side of Turkey's current account external balance). Increased trade with as many nations as possible indicates diversification for Turkey's exports. When a nation's trading associations are limited, it is vulnerable to changes in any one nation's economy and trade policies. Therefore, when the export markets are diversified, Turkey is less vulnerable yet interdependent as are other nations. The level of interdependence is, however, increased and diversified; it assumes that all the trading associates will not change policies and create disruptions within the same time-frame as they are impacted by regionalization and globalization.

Regionalization, as exemplified by the EU, is driven by political forces of states with economic concerns. The objectives of the member states are to enhance member states' growth by reducing intra-regional barriers for the purpose of moving goods, money and labor forces across borders. A specific internal objective of states in joining a regional organization may be to disrupt the tendency of entrenched groups to retard economic growth. This tendency to limit the capacity of states for adopting new technologies, and increasing barriers to market regulations, can be upset by the policies of a regional organization. For example, the EU's purpose is to eliminate barriers to the flow of trade and to set specific standards for production. It is often necessary to weaken or upset these internal entrenched groups in order to stimulate competition and growth (Osman 1994, 34).

The entrenched SEEs in Turkey, by OECD recommendation, have traveled the difficult course to privatization. In the case of its current customs union status with the EU, Turkey has a common external trade policy with the member nations. Regionalization strengthens member growth and enhances the possibility for extra-regional trade and investment. In this latter sense, it shares similarities with globalization in that it can be facilitated by government policies which decrease barriers to trade and investment.

Although globalization is driven by microeconomic forces and regionalization by political and economic forces, they are not antithetical. Both regionalization and globalization are reinforcing when regional integration assists in strengthening market competition within specific regions (Osman 1994, 11-34). Regionalization at the separate state micro-economic level is a power surge to the globalization process, which in turn may challenge regional growth. Regionalization challenges developing nations to meet standards, to specialize, to improve the quality of their products for export, and to integrate their political and economic structures with the demands of the established regional organization.

Globalization is a phenomenon proportional to the level of integration and competitiveness of markets. Globalization results from increased integration within regionalization because integrated states within a regional organization are involved in specialization and competition. Integration, regionalization, specialization and competition are responsible for the phenomenon referred to as globalization. The structure of firms, and their continual quest for specialization and involvement in the mode of production, regulate capital accumulation. Therefore, Turkey as a middle-income state has determined that the level of integration into the EU is proportional to its (Turkey's) capacity to increase product specialization, economies of scale, intra-industry trade, and thereby accumulating capital. Intra-industry trade is usually highest in the iron and steel industry followed by non-ferrous metals, rubber products, ceramics and glass. Turkey, involved in manufacturing these products, can improve its level of production by meeting EU regional standards. Meeting these EU standards increases the competitive level of products and in turn improves firms, their productive capacities and market shares.

The observable inequitable developed, developing, and less-developed divisions increasingly explain the unchallenged capitalist system as the source of the globalization process. This globalization process continues to progress as economic and political integration and regionalization expand and as transition economies (former Soviet system and East Europe) change to the capitalist market system. The EU as an integrated regionalized political, economic and social organization promotes interdependence among the inequitable divisions of nations through their specialized market system. In other words, product specialization means that nation's firms focus on a few specialized products and depend on other nations for the products they need but do not produce.

Turkey as a developing nation contributes to the ever-increasing globalization process in several specific ways: economic integration into the EU through the customs union and the OECD (the majority of the EU and OECD nations belong to the core, high income nations); World Trade Organization membership; NATO membership; and the recent alliance with Israel. As a middle-income nation geographically situated in both the Middle East and Europe, Turkey is interacting with the European nations, the Middle Eastern Arab nations, and the Central Asian states.

Returning to the account balances, in addition to the EU examination of the external current account balances for membership candidacy, the internal balance is also reviewed. The internal balance refers to the goal of a fully employed economy and keeping inflation as low as possible. The Turkish economy experienced a period between 1995 and 1998 in which the GDP averaged over seven and five-tenths percent in 1997 and eight and seven-tenths percent in the first quarter of 1998 (OECD 1999, 25). However, inflation has continued to be a problem as a result of excessive public spending. Inflation distorts the level of investment and savings. It also affects favorable supply-side economic activity. In an open capitalist market, inflation usually means high interest rates. Turkey's inflation has created a currency substitution situation in the use of foreign money. In this situation Turkish export firms have learned that the use of foreign currency is advantageous in dealing with the problem of exchange rate depreciation. In other words, these export firms deal in foreign currency rather than going through the process of exchanging Turkish liras for the foreign currency needed for transactions. Also the exporting firms are effective in terms of borrowing. With foreign bank (joint stock companies and branches from abroad) access in Turkey, foreign currency can be readily obtained by Turkish export firms.

Small to medium-sized non-exporting firms usually have to resort to their own funds for financing. These problems in part stem from the fact that the largest private banks belong to families which provide loans principally to firms, organizations or customers with established credit credentials and records. Thus the banking system has become dependent on risk-free income, yet creating the inefficient distribution of resources to selective customers. Another banking problem exists with state banks granting subsidized loans to favored groups. These banks usually lack sufficient capital from the treasury to deal with losses.

This situation can cause cash-flow difficulty and in turn a liability to the government (OECD 1999, 126-127).

Banks in Turkey have followed the political development trends that began with the establishment of the secular republic in 1923. The first National Economic Congress decided that banks would be established to finance principal sectors of the economy and a Central Bank for regulatory purposes. With the policy of etatism in effect, six state banks were established and remained effective after 1950. Thereafter, etatism was replaced by the beginning stages of private sector policies, the expansion of international cooperative efforts and the establishment of private banks. This was the era of the beginning of Turkey's multiparty system and the Menderes regime. The 1960s ushered in a semi-return to planned development with the state commanding the public sector and recommending policies for the private sector.

This planned development began with the well-known five-year plans endemic to state-controlled economies. As late as 1980, liberalized economic policies focused on the establishment of a free-market economy and integration with the global economy. This period ushered in structural, legal and institutional developments in Turkey's banking system. Reforms were designed to promote financial markets and to increase the efficiency of the economic system by supporting competitiveness in banking. Competition among banks permitted the flotation of interest and foreign exchange rates. The liberalized economic policies welcomed foreign banks to open their branches in Turkey. By 1985, the establishment of all Turkish banks was according to authorization granted by the Council of Ministers and Banking Law #3182. In order for foreign banks to be established, they must have the permission of the Council of Ministries; they must sell their capital to the Central Bank of Turkey.[3]

The liberalization of the economy of foreign exchange regulations increased foreign banking transactions. By 1986 the Interbank Money Market was established to regulate the liquidity of funds for banks. The adoption of uniform accounting practices and a standardized reporting system facilitated and integrated procedures in international banking transactions. The standardized uniform practices extended to bank audits by external independent auditors. Within the same time-frame of international standardized banking procedures, capital markets were developed according to legal and international policies. Development of capital markets was accompanied by diversification of products and services.

The EU and OECD examination of Turkey's banks revealed sufficient and positive information in terms of preparation for EU membership candidacy. The information may also be supportive in terms of the external continual recommendations for privatization of state owned banks and firms. In September of 1995 when Turkey was granted customs union status, shares of the three major types of banks in Turkey revealed the following: state banks, twenty-two percent; national private banks, sixty-six percent; and foreign banks, twelve percent of the total profits. If comparisons are made between the state and private banks with respect to their profits and deposits, the private banks appear to be more entrepreneurial. For example, the private banks collect around fifty-three percent of the total deposits with total profits of sixty-six percent, whereas the state banks collect forty-seven percent of the total deposits with total profits of twenty-two percent (see OECD 1995 report). These percentages reveal that the private banks demonstrate a significantly wider margin of total profits to deposit ratio over the state banks profit to deposit ratio.

Usually the banking sector of any economy is vulnerable during periods of adjustments. Therefore, the OECD has recommended the establishment of an independent regulatory and supervisory board for Turkey. These recommendations go beyond the current Central Bank and Treasury shared responsibilities by suggesting the need for external objective evaluative criteria rather than the internal subjective system currently in effect. The OECD has specifically focused on a select external supervisory board with the capacity to effectively and objectively evaluate each division within Turkey's banking system. The OECD, through observation and the examination of comparative data, has noted that privatization of Turkey's state banks has yielded improved efficiency (OECD 1999, 127). Published OECD reports concerning the economic status of Turkey in both internal and external interaction, productivity, management, and the capacity to follow recommended procedures for improved growth, have been positive and important to the EU Commission. These reports should be acknowledged by Turkish government officials who consistently maintain that EU membership has been delayed for political reasons. For example, in 1998 before the EU had accepted Turkey for membership candidacy, Gazi Ercel, governor of the Central Bank, delivered a speech at the CBRT conference hall informing the public of these political reasons. He said that "economic issues have taken second place in Turkey-EU relations; that the subject of inflation should be examined."[4] The OECD published reports however, have specifically addressed the problem of inflation accompanied by recommendations. Therefore, a focused attention on the political issues by the Central Bank governor without acknowledging the OECD reports, misinforms the Turkish public. Indeed, the EU has consistently referred to the Cyprus, Greek and Kurdish problems; however, recognition of economic improvements through OECD assistance and recommendations has not been sufficiently acknowledged by Turkish authorities and officials.[5]

Turkey's budget deficit also reflects the internal balance of the economic criteria necessary for EU membership. The OECD is concerned with correcting defects in Turkey's structure. The 1998-1999 tax reforms focused on personal and capital income taxation, corporate taxation and tax administration. One problem undermining income tax reform has been the concern to protect Turkish taxpayers from the inequities of inflation. An inflation index adjustment has been implemented on the basis of income tax levels and requirements for exemptions. Another concern is the deficient number of citizens filing tax forms as evidenced by the collection rate (on average, around 89.5 percent of the total assessments).

In order to simplify the problem of tax collecting and administration and to defer the problem of criminal implication for tax evasion, the government launched the Financial Millennium. The Millennium acted as a pardon, an amnesty, yet an attempt to collect revenue to assist in financing the budget deficits. A temporary program during 1998, the Millennium allowed citizens with undisclosed funds to bring this money to banks. According to OECD findings, this one-year program broadened the tax base and accounted for the establishment of new corporations and an increase in foreign exchange deposits (OECD 1999, 66-69).

By 1998, eleven million tax identification numbers had been assigned to Turkish citizens. This registration represented an increase of twice the number over the previous year. 1998 was also a year for dealing with the sluggish provincial areas which had limited links with the General Directorate of Revenue at the national level. The GDR as a representative of the Ministry of Finance is responsible for tax laws and collecting and auditing procedures. With the establishment of regional auditing centers reporting to the GDR, another improvement in tax administration was enacted (OECD 1999, 66-69).

Prior to the EU acceptance of Turkey as a candidate for membership, the past two years indicated areas of improvement acknowledged by the review Commission.

Registered employment had risen by two and eight tenths percent and the trade deficit decreased to seven and one tenths percent of the GDP. The current account changed from a one and four tenths percent deficit to a surplus of six and nine tenths percent of the GDP. The most notable improvement was the significant decline in inflation from one hundred one and six tenths percent to sixty four and three tenths percent. Regarding fiscal policies, the Turkish government reduced expenditures and implemented tax laws. Privatization continued by selling state-dominated companies in oil, iron, steel, the chemical industries, the airlines and a few state banks. The establishment of regulatory and supervisory boards has also improved banking operations (OECD 1997-1999 reports).

# Political Criteria for EU Membership

The EU's examination of the current political situation in Turkey registered some reservations and approvals. On the approval side, the Demirel/Ecevit coalition government was skillful in dealing with opposition parties in the parliament (Grand National Assembly). After five governments had collapsed since 1995, a coalition government was finally approved on June 9, 1999. This coalition government, lead by Prime Minister Bulent Ecevit and his Democratic Left Party (DSP) shared power with the Nationalist Movement Party (MHP) and the Motherland Party (ANAP). The two parties with the highest percentage of the votes, the DSP and the MHP, have traditionally been rivals, however; they shared a continued interest in the modernization and secularization of Turkey. This interest in modernization and secularization is also shared by the military, the self-appointed watchdog of the Atatürk legacy of the secularized Turkish Republic.

The military, well-informed and appraised of Ecevit's policies, supported and approved the coalition government and the skill Ecevit employed in demonstrating the importance of collaborative, cooperative democratic government. The pervasive influence of the military, established by Atatürk's legacy, has continued through times of political instability and stability. Army generals, briefed each month by political leaders, contribute recommendations which are usually accepted by the government. After the previous four years of weak coalition governments, military threats, and the apparent political strength demonstrated by Islamic parties and government corruption, the June 1999 votes of confidence for Ecevit and the DSP seemed promising.

On April 18, 1999, prior to confirmation of the coalition government, citizens of Turkey had voted for the parties awarded the highest votes. With a choice of twenty-one different parties, the Turkish voters seemed to cast responses against the perils of the previous weakly-formed coalitions, the corruption and lack of party cohesion for policy objectives. Instead of casting votes for many different parties, the voters concentrated on three parties and three leaders who had not been charged or associated with corrupt practices in government. The voters also seemed to be concerned with selections that might appease the military's committed support for secular political parties. Perhaps the voters are sufficiently cognizant of the fact that casting a majority of votes for an Islamic affiliated party will inevitably not only cause conflict with secular government policies, but will also increase the possibility of military intervention. Although the Islamic Virtue Party did not receive the sufficient percentage required for a coalition government, this party has not been banned from parliament. Rather, the Virtue Party has been protected by the Political Parties Law which allows it to continue as a party. This measure taken by the government to prevent the banning of the Virtue Party is an expression of tolerance. It is also an indication of the skill Ecevit exercised in working with the Virtue Party, parliament's main opposition in terms of policy agreement.

The parliament in the constitution of the Republic of Turkey is referred to as the Grand National Assembly, the legislative body comprised of five hundred and fifty deputies elected by Turkish voters (see constitution, part three, articles 75-76, Appendix II). The GNA/parliament elects the president from among its own members (see constitution, part three, article 101, Appendix II). Suleyman Demirel, as former head of state appointed Ecevit as Prime Minister and leader of the DSP, the party receiving the highest number of votes from the general populace. In turn, Prime Minister Ecevit nominated the ministers who together formed the Council of Ministers, part of the executive division of government (see constitution, part three, articles 109-116, Appendix II).

One of the disadvantages of Turkey's parliamentary system had been evident from 1995 until June of 1999. With no one party holding a majority of the seats, weak coalitions created an unstable government. In attempting to form coalitions, finally to secure a majority vote of confidence, the parties involved are often in disagreement. These disagreements result in lack of cooperation for the enactment of government objectives and implementation of policies for effective government. Moreover, the party coalitions divide the task of selecting the Council of Ministers, which may pursue different objectives. Continual disagreements may cause parliament to become paralyzed; the government may temporarily collapse and a new coalition must be negotiated and/or the military steps in as an interim care-taker of the government.

The advantages of a parliamentary system of government are evident. If there is a one-party majority or a unified effective coalition, the government can respond to issues and problems more directly than in a fragmented system. Another advantage of the parliamentary system is party-line accountability. Once the party, or a unified coalition is in power, the general populace is aware of policy fulfillment or lack of the enactment of promised policies. Thus policies and party promises are easily traced and identified within the parliamentary system of government. The Ecevit coalition government successfully passed legislation based upon IMF recommendations for inflation control, continued privatization programs and foreign direct investment. These measures, passed after Ecevit's coalition government had been in power only ten weeks, marked the beginnings of an effective government Turkey had not experienced since Ozal's 1980 government. The capability of the seasoned politician Ecevit, was undoubtedly noted by the EU Commission when the December 1999 decision in Helsinki confirmed Turkey's status as a candidate for membership.

The EU Commission remains concerned by the influence the National Security Council continues to exercise in Turkey's political affairs. Article 118 of the Constitution requests that the NSC submit proposals for the establishment and implementation of policies related to the state and its national security. These proposals are submitted to the Council of Ministers, which is required to review them for primary consideration and policy formation (see constitution, part three, article 118, Appendix II). During the preparation period for full EU membership, article 118 of the Turkish Constitution may emerge as an area for examination and subject to questioning. Other areas subject to examination are: the human rights issues related to the Kurdish problems; the necessity to seek a resolution to the Greek/Cyprus issue; the maintenance of political stability during coalition governments; and continued economic improvements. The positive areas of progress have been: the political skills exercised by a coalition government indicating government stability; removal of the veto power exercised by Greece against Turkey's EU candidacy; and continual, yet slow economic progress, according to the OECD reports.

By European and western standards, nations experiencing military coups represent political instability and an inability to exercise the democratic processes of government. Turkey, however, has a legacy of military heroes who after military service have been elected to political office. These former military heroes, after attaining public office, have been instrumental in initiating and supporting the process of a secular republic with a multiparty system. Atatürk, a military hero, established the secular republic; Inonu, also a respected military hero, initiated the multiparty system, instituted by 1950. Each of the three military coups was an emergency situation requiring administrative skills that either corrupt leaders or weak coalition governments were previously unable to provide. By comparative standards (in terms of the length of time the democratic processes have been functioning in the western and European worlds), Turkey is a relative new parliamentary republic. Therefore, a military legacy inspired by dedication and service to the Republic of Turkey is in conflict with the anti-militaristic rationale empowering the establishment of the EU. The well-regulated EU rejects any affiliation of its members with anti-human rights or anti-Semitic activities. Radical political parties gaining political power, or military interference in the government structure of EU members, violates the philosophical basis of the EU's foundation. The EU's recent rejection of Austria's radical Freedom Party sends a clear message to Turkey and other nations intent upon EU membership, that undemocratic behavior will not be tolerated.

The Freedom Party, headed by a Nazi devotee who is against immigrants in Austria, won the second highest percentage of votes in the October 1999 election.[6] As a result of the votes cast for this anti-immigrant Nazi affiliated party, the EU reduced diplomatic ties with Austria. As a result of the world-wide reaction against the Freedom Party, the leader, Joerg Haider, resigned his parliament seat. The apparent message from the EU not only to Austria, but also to potential and current members is: nondemocratic activity will not be tolerated. The military coups in Turkey have been perceived by the EU as nondemocratic. However, the composition and capacity of Turkey's parliament has been positively accepted by the EU Commission. The second message from the EU to those nations who have viewed their membership status negatively is: all potential members must meet and continue to demonstrate acceptable economic, political and social EU membership criteria or they, like Austria, will experience rejection.

Former rejections for membership were not only based upon political and economic criteria Turkey had failed to meet, but also the veto power Greece (up until December of 1999) had exercised against Turkey. Moreover, human rights issues denied the Kurds, and the Turkish/Cypriot division of Cyprus remain irreconciled issues. Thus the common belief that Turkey had been rejected on the grounds of religious and cultural differences with Europe seemed to disappear when the EU Commission issued the December 1999 conditional membership invitation. The EU Commission, aware that the Islamic *Fazilat Partisi* currently holds seats in parliament, has not rejected Turkey for membership as a result of this cultural, Islamic and political identification. These reasons which Turkey has internalized as confirmations of its previous rejections for membership into the EU, were not substantiated when the Helsinki deliberations issued Turkey an invitation to membership candidacy. All nations, part of a regional political economic and social organization, in order to achieve and maintain membership, are required to abide by the rules and regulations providing privileges to its membership. While the EU enables its constituency, it also constrains and regulates the economic and political activities of its members. If nations elect to depart from the EU agreements, then the degree of departure could become proportional to gradual disintegration within the EU. Integrated EU membership is continual on the basis of agreement and cooperation to uphold democratic principles and economic regulations.

The EU's suspension of bilateral relations with Austria, as a result of Austrian support for the radical Freedom Party, was a rejection of the nondemocratic exercise of political power at the national level within the context of the larger EU organization. The EU clearly fears that the exercise of governmental authority by neo-fascists in Austria or the politicization of the military in Turkey can threaten the democratic principles of the entire organization. The contexts of the exercise of non-democratic power in Austria and Turkey are entirely different and not comparable in terms of a military legacy vested in Turkey's constitution versus the rise to secondary power of the radical Austrian Freedom Party. There is, however, the possibility for a comparison between the Freedom Party's position against immigrants in Austria and Turkey's treatment of Kurds as outside the mainstream of Turkish citizenship. Both Austrian and Turkish reactions to a segment of their population considered non-integrated and threatening, could be classified as unacceptable to the EU's human rights charter. The EU, on each review of Turkey's request for membership, has cited the necessity to resolve the Kurdish problem before enacting or confirming its candidacy status. Similarly, the EU has denounced Austria's Freedom Party for intolerant and undemocratic behavior aimed against the large immigrant population.

If Turkish Prime Minister Recep Erdoğan is separated from Islamic party affiliations, and exercises democratic government skills, there should be limited reason for government demise and/or subsequent military intervention. Conversely, if in the future Turkey experiences military intervention in governmental affairs, the EU may again postpone membership (assuming that military action would occur before the finalized acceptance into membership). Despite the legacy of an emergency care-taker government devoted to preserving the legacy of a secular democratic government established by a military hero, civilian control of a nation's government is a measurable criterion for democratic government stability. The EU has its own system for measuring a potential candidate for membership. The EU's political measurement criteria for examining Turkey prior to membership candidacy status was conducted in October of 1999. The EU's examination of Turkey's political level of democracy and the Rule of Law appear to be satisfactory. The power vested in the National Security Council, however, remains questionable. In the areas of human rights and the protection of minorities, civil and political rights and protection instruments were examined. From eighteen categories established by the Human Rights Convention, Turkey has as of June, 1999, ratified only four (see Appendix VI).

# Conclusion for Chapter 6

Economic integration is the process of eliminating restrictions to international trade and payments. The step-by-step procedures toward integration usually begin with free trade areas and are accompanied by a customs union, common market, economic union, and finally a monetary union. States with full membership in the EU are recipients of all the benefits of those step-by-step procedures; however, the last step, a monetary union with a common currency (the Euro), is a relatively recent step for even the original members. Thus Turkey, with its status as a conditional EU member, is at the second stage of economic integration. This status has advantages in that Turkey has time to adjust to the increasing EU restrictions and regulations imposed with each stage of economic integration. Turkey also has the advantage of noting the adjustments other states encountered as they experienced each stage; and as they are now accommodating usage of the Euro currency. As economic integration advances, a very important consideration for Turkey will be the flexibility of its market interaction with Central Asia.

Although accepted as a conditional candidate, Turkey is, in terms of step-by-step integration into the EU, at the initial customs union stage. Currently, this level of integration means that Turkey trades with the EU members on a tariff-free basis. It also means that Turkey has latitude concerning its trading policies with non-EU members. This is important in terms of Turkey's trade with less developed nations unable to trade with core nations. By focusing on trade liberalization policies (recommended by the OECD and beginning in the 1980s), Turkey was able to off-set the imbalance between exports and imports. This initial effort was the beginning of a steady (yet at times interrupted) movement toward plans for EU membership.

According to the political and economic criteria established by the EU, Turkey continues to be successful as a conditional candidate for membership. Turkey, in an effort to indicate its viable potential to trade in the competitive global markets, increased manufactured products to a twenty-nine percent share in 1980, and to a sixty-nine percent share in 1991. Although revitalized Islam, by entering the political structure of parliament (through legitimized, resurrected political parties), has periodically derailed Turkey's secular objectives, government stability has been maintained since the 1980 military coup. The Ecevit and Demirel secular administration exhibited skills in initiating and passing legislation important to Turkey's political and economic standing with the EU. Voter dissatisfaction with the Ecevit and Demirel government caused a party change on November 3rd of 2002. Thus the Justice and Development party (AKP), by winning the majority vote in the 2002 November election, is led by: Prime Minister Recep Erdoğan, President Ahmet Sezer, and Foreign Minister Abdullah Gül. This leadership continues preparations recommended for Turkey's full EU membership to be reviewed during the 2007 June EU Summit meetings.

# Notes

1. The Institutions of the European Union, beginning in 1957, were created to enhance a networked Union of European nations. As new members have been accepted, the Union's responsibilities have expanded and the institutions have become larger and new ones have been added. During the first twenty years, the Commission proposed ideas and legislation, the Parliament advised, the Council of Ministers made decisions and the Court of Justice interpreted those decisions.

   a. The Parliament represents the 370 million citizens of the Union, its primary objectives are to pass sound laws and to scrutinize and control the use of executive power. Its powers have been strengthened by the Single Act of 1987 and by the Treaty of European Union in 1993.
   b. The Council is a body with the characteristics of both a supranational and inter governmental organization, deciding some matters by qualified majority voting, and others by unanimity. In its procedures, its customs and practices, and even in its disputes, the Council depends on a degree of solidarity and trust.
   c. The role and responsibilities of the European Commission place it at the heart of the European Union's policy-making process. In some respects, it seems to be the source from which other institutions derive their purpose.
   d. The Success of Community law is due to having been perceived, interpreted and applied by the citizens, the administrative authorities and the courts of all of the Member States. The Community laws are uniform rules upon which individuals may rely in their national courts. The decisions of the Court have Community law a reality for the citizens of Europe and often have important constitutional and economic consequences.

e.   The European Court of Auditors is referred to as the "financial con-
     science" of the Union. It is a guarantor that certain moral, adminis-
     trative and accounting principles will be respected. The Court's re-
     ports are source of information on the management of the Union's
     finances, and a source of pressure on the institutions with manage-
     ment responsibility.
f.   The European Investment Bank is a flexible and cost-effective source
     of finance whose 33 billion EURO volume of annual lending makes it
     the largest international financing institution in the world.
g.   The Economic and Social Committee consists of workers, employers
     and a variety of interests who write opinions and draft Community
     legislation on the main issues affecting society. Thus they represent
     the various sectors of civil society.
h.   The Committee of the Regions makes it a legal obligation to consult
     the representatives of local and regional authorities on a variety of
     matters directly concerning them.
i.   The Ombudsman has the power to request all documents and evi-
     dence from member nations and their national authorities. He may
     act as a conciliator between citizens and Community administration.
     He can make recommendations to EC insituations and refer the case
     to the European Parliament so that the latter can draw political con-
     clusions from the attitude taken by the administration. Within the last
     twenty years, the Parliament has become directly-elected and acquired
     new powers, the Court of Auditors is new and the European Invest-
     ment Bank has emerged as a major source of finance for economic
     development. The newer institutions have been set up to advance
     regional interests and diversity (http://europa.eu.int/ inst-en.htm)

2. In 1999 all members of the European Union were preparing for the
common money, the EURO to be the medium of exchange. In addition to a
central bank, each region, and each city with all of its markets and stores were
preparing for the advent of the EURO. This researcher observed that all prices
on all items for sale in the state of Germany, for example, were marked by the
German mark and the new EURO. This method allowed the citizens to familiarize themselves with the value of the EURO compared with their own
currencies.

3. All banks in Turkey are subject to Banking Law #.3182 of 1985. The
establishment of a bank depends on authorization given by the Council of
Ministers. For a new bank to be established, it must be a joint-stock company
with a minimum of TL one trillion worth of total paid-up capital. Opening of
new branch banks is restricted to ten in a calendar year. To open more than
ten, requires the permission of the Undersecretary of Foreign Trade. Foreign
banks can operate in Turkey by establishing a branch or subsidiary or by

going into a joint venture with an established bank. Foreign banks must bring their capital allocated to Turkey in foreign exchange and sell it to the Central Bank of the Republic of Turkey. The legal framework concerning the functioning of foreign banks in Turkey is the same as that regulating domestic banks (http://www.turkey.org/business/bank.htm).

4. Gazi Ercel, Governor of the Central Bank of the Republic of Turkey, in a seminar speech on the European Political Union and Turkey, stated that "the idea of economic solidarity that emerged from the structural differences of societies at the beginning of the 20th century flourished first on a bilateral basis, before leading countries to establish larger supranational economic organizations whose goal was cooperation with one another." "Political cooperation is one of the most important aspects of regional integration; it contributes to economic development by supporting mutual removal of trade barriers." He believes that political debates have come to dominate EU-Turkey relations. "Such political issues as Cyprus, the Aegean Sea, Turkish-Greek relations, and problems in Southeastern Turkey (read Kurds) have dominated the agenda." Ercel has complained that the economic subject of inflation has little attention or how the EU can help Turkey with this problem. "The agenda of Turkey-EU relations have always moved in the opposite direction from the EU's own agenda. While the EU was focusing on economic subjects, we were focusing on political issues, and when they began to concern themselves with the idea of political union, we preferred to focus on other areas not connected with politics." (http://www.tcmb.gov.tr/yeni/evds/konsuma/ing/1998/europel.htm)

5. Amidst a large gathering of 150,000 Austrians protesting the Freedom Party and its leader, Joerg Haider, Hans Marschalek, head of the inmates association from Austria's Mauthausen concentration camp spoke decisively. "We have to prevent right-wing nationalism from creeping into Austria again." Haider is opposed to immigration, rapid European Union expansion, and has praised Nazi policies. As a result of Haider and his Freedom Party's positions, the EU, Israel and the US have taken measures to isolate Austria diplomatically. These measures, as well as Austrians against Haider, have resulted in his resignation.

6. The human rights situation in Turkey is still under the monitoring procedures opened in 1996 by the Council of Europe. An information report on "Honoring of obligations and commitments by Turkey" has been published in January 1999. The EU's Commission on the progress towards Turkey's membership has noted deficits in the following areas: Cases of harassment and police violence against individual journalists are still being reported by international human rights organizations; Overpopulation and lack of adequate medical care remain major problems in Turkish prisons; freedom of association and assembly continue to be subject to limitations; and regarding freedom of religion, there still exists a difference of treatment between those

religious minorities recognized by the Lausanne Treaty and other religious minorities. Positive developments include the lifting of reservations against the UN Convention for the elimination of all forms of discrimination against women. President Demirel approved a law postponing prosecutions and punishment for offenses committed through the press and broadcasting (sentences can be suspended for a three-year parole period). As far as extra-judicial executions are concerned, the Constitutional Court annulled a legal provision in 1999, which entitled security officers to "fire directly and without hesitation at persons who do not stop when warned." The government has been given one year to prepare a new legal provision to replace the old one. In the aftermath of the Ocalan capture, the Minister of Justice issued a communiqué to Governors to identify associations, foundations, publications, individuals or organizations likely to favor Ocalan. Since this writing, the EU has warned Turkey against executing Ocalan. (http://europa.eu.int/comm/enlargement/turkey/rep_10_99/b23.htm)

# Chapter 7

## Conclusions

This research has focused on the case study of Turkey, a middle-income nation impacted by exogenous forces that have encouraged political and socio-economic institutional transformation. The research has linked a nation state to the international system by examining the recommendations of external agents capable of influencing Turkey to pass legislation for internal institutional restructuring. The independent variable, nation state interdependence affected and continues to affect Turkey's economic and political structures in significant ways. Increased specialization and globalization of international markets demand that separate nation states produce competitive goods and services. In order to concentrate on competitive specialized goods and services, Turkey adhered to OECD and EU standardization and competitive procedures, and it applied them to industrial products such as iron, steel, chemicals, textiles, machinery and clothing (see Appendix V). Additionally, Turkey reduced its number of exportable goods similar to those produced in other nations also specializing and competing in the globalized markets. This focus and concentration improved the balance of payments and awakened Turkey not only to the realization that EU membership required an improved economy measurable by international criteria; but also to the understanding that political stability and government efficiency were essential. Those international agents perpetuating interdependence were also involved in extensive recommendations for privatization of Turkey's state-controlled SEEs and for a detailed social security program.

The two principal assertions of the research are: exogenous globalized forces in the interdependent system of nations have impacted

Turkey's political and socio-economic institutions, and Turkey has encountered difficulties in restructuring its institutions to accommodate those forces. All interdependent states functioning within global capitalist markets intensifies the need for any state to seek membership in and/or affiliation with international organizations promoting relatively tariff-free access for exports and imports. This research has revealed that interaction with more developed nations and their organizations has increased Turkey's capacity for product specialization and market shares. Its economic, political, and social interaction with more developed nations has been strengthened through international organizations and their capitalist markets. Turkey's advancement from a less-developed to a developing state is the result of its progressive interaction with developed nations. Its secularized political and social institutions have facilitated the process of adjusting to external political and economic pressures and forces acting on global organizations and markets.

Turkey's political institutions had been impacted by Atatürk's Europeanized reforms adopted in 1923. Following the establishment of the Turkish Republic, a two-party system initiated the democratization of the electoral process. The reforms implemented by Atatürk and his military officials were dedicated to transforming Turkey into a secular republic with a legal system conformable to European law. Beginning in 1963, recommendations from the OECD assisted Turkey in improving its economy, and confidence in the political system increased when Turgut Ozal became prime minister in 1983. Ozal's accomplishments, discussed in Chapter 3, reflected the impact of European democratic concepts. His publications regarding cooperation between Europe and Turkey, and the privatization of state industry as recommended by the OECD, assisted in the gradual programmatic and institutional changes Turkey accepted as necessary for EU membership. The 1980-1999 OECD publications indicated extensive continual recommendations for privatization of the SEEs and enactment of a comprehensive social security program. These recommendations were reflected in legislation passed by Prime Minister Ecevit in August of 1999. The political capacity to act on these exogenous forces impacting Turkey's institutions became proportional to government stability, effective coalitions, and lack of threats or interference from the military and Islamic parties.

The research demonstrates that Turkey has become serious about the necessity to comply with OECD recommendations and EU criteria for membership. Since 1980, Turkey has avoided military intervention by: (1) exercising political competence in forming necessary coalitions; (2) accommodating opposition parties in decisions (3) implementing OECD, IMF and EU recommendations by privatizing its SEEs, improving its social security program, passing legislation for foreign investment policies; (4) and partially complying with EU membership criteria for improving its human rights record (see Appendix VI). The 1999 appointment of Prime Minister Bulent Ecevit sent a signal to the EU that Turkey was serious about EU membership and European identity. Within four months after it successfully passed OECD and IMF economic recommendations, the EU announced that Turkey was a candidate for conditional membership. This membership status will again be reviewed in 2004.

Four intervening variables causing Turkey to be derailed from realizing its major objectives have been Islamic parties, the Kurdish problem, threats of military intervention and global economic shifts. The administration of Prime Minister Ecevit and President Demirel was successful in accommodating Islamic parties formerly outlawed by the 1982 constitution. This administration's use of power was accepted by leaders of the Islamic parties, the populace, and even the military. These seasoned politicians possessed the political skill and power needed to satisfy Islamic parties and the military watch-dogs of the secular republic. Ecevit skillfully sought the support and cooperation of Islamic parties in parliament when he successfully passed the August 1999 OECD and IMF recommended legislation. This success indicates Turkey's compliance with the exogenous forces vested in the OECD. Since the EU Human Rights Charter stipulates that Ocalan, the leader of the Kurdish Workers Party cannot be executed, Turkey must reconsider its legal adherence to specific articles of its constitution (see part one, articles 14 & 15, Appendix II). A third intervening variable, military intervention by a coup, derailed Turkey in 1980. Although a subsequent threat existed in 1997, the Islamic party leader, Erbakan, resigned to prevent military involvement in Turkey's civilian political institutions. Again, Turkey is confronted with the resurgence of Islamic party identity in the leader Recep Erdoğan, representing the Justice and Development Party (AKP), and voted into power in the November 2002 election. The complexity of this election may present conflicts for Turkey, now that the Islamic affiliated leadership of the Justice and Development Party received the necessary majority, entitling and enabling it to form a parliamentary government without relying on a coalition. Perhaps the conflict involves the reluctance of the military, opposed to Islamic party affiliations, to intervene now that the Justice and Development party has won this significant majority. The conflict may also involve the current administration's awareness that the EU membership committee might view any Islamic party affiliation as undemocratic, regardless of Erdoğan's declaration that he no longer retains affiliations that represent Muslim or Islamic ties.

The fourth intervening variable, economic shifts during 1980-1999, has caused difficulty for Turkey as it has confronted the policies of etatism and privatization of state-controlled enterprises according to OECD recommendations, and more recently, the World Bank decision that state effectiveness and intervention should be considered in cases where industries were under-performing; but that industries should be privatized when performing at or near capacity. Determining the direction for these industries, as recommended by the World Bank, has been assisted by parliamentary legislation passed in August of 1999. This legislation, discussed in Chapter 3, permits foreign investment in Turkey's economic institutions.

My research demonstrates the utility of the theoretical perspectives of interdependence and pluralism in explaining Turkey's interaction with international organizations. Interdependence between developing and developed states has exposed Turkey to relatively higher levels of sensitivity and vulnerability. Turkey has experienced sensitivity as a result of transaction costs associated with the ongoing process of privatizing its SEEs. Turkey has also considered its level of vulnerability when exposed to transaction costs exceeding its capacity to transform the SEEs, and when trading partners are limited. OECD input, assistance, and recommendations have been influential in surpassing anticipated levels of vulnerability as Turkey continues to respond to those influences.

My research also indicates that the theoretical perspective of pluralism is useful for explaining changes in Turkey's internal political, economic and social policies. The political structures have held together coalition governments; parliament has accommodated Islamic parties; has prevented military intervention since 1980; and has passed previously cited legislation recommended by the OECD. EU candidacy status and OECD assistance have facilitated Turkey's access to highly competitive international capitalist markets. If Turkey subscribes to the demands of the EU regarding the human rights of the Kurdish population and improved Greek/Turkish relations, a further step toward democratizing its internal policies, as stipulated by the EU, could be accomplished.

The findings discredit the Huntington thesis that Turkey's political and economic structures are Islamic; that it should be identified with the Middle East; and that it should not be classified or identified with Europe or the west. Although Turkey has an Islamic cultural heritage, its secular political structures have been recognized by the OECD and the EU. Moreover, membership in NATO, its alliances with Israel, and its recent EU candidacy status, contradict Huntington's thesis. Islamic party identity or affiliation with any one of Turkey's political parties by elected leaders who either resign or denounce pro Islamic policies, does not signal a threat to the stability of Turkey's republic. If an Islamic party were in power, rather than the current Justice and Development party, then there would be cause for concern.

The EU Summit in June of 2007 discussed a revised constitution for improving EU decision-making processes to include the new positions of president, rather than the curent six month rotational system, and foreign minister. In 2005, this proposed constitution was rejected by French and Dutch voters. Two years later, this constitution, now referred to as a reform treaty, has been reviewed and accepted by the twenty-seven members who also reviewed a plan for regulating country voting power to begin in 2014, and to be implemented by 2017. The current voting rights and power of each EU country is vested in its population. If the voting power continues to be based upon the population of each EU member, then Turkey, if accepted into membership, would have comparable voting power with Germany, an issue of concern for some long-standing members.

After the rotating EU presidential term of Chancellor Angela Merkel expired, Portugal's Prime Minister, Jose Socrates took office for six months on July 1, 2007. President Socrates disagrees with France's President Nicolas Sarkosy regarding Turkey's EU candidacy status. President Sarkosy has attempted to influence EU members that Turkey should join a Mediterranean union; however, President Socrates supports Turkey's EU candidacy status, to be reviewed for the next six month period. President Socrates views Turkey's future membership as vital to the geographical region. Moreover, President Socrates acknowledges the difficult membership process Portugal experienced, and the benefits accrued during the accession to membership. Will the

EU members view Turkey as "the rest of Europe" during the crucial discussions for accession to membership, scheduled for implementation by the year 2015? There are thirty-five *acquis communautaire* (EU legal requirements) to be met by any country aspiring to EU membership. Thus Turkey must fulfill the remaining unmet *acquis*, criteria, and with external assistance, resolve the Kurdish and Cyprus issues during the period before the established accession date.

# Appendix I

## Journal Critiques of Wallerstein's World System

### First Critique

Journal: *International Studies Quarterly* (1988) 32, 47-65)
Article: "The Brenner-Wallerstein Debate" by Robert A. Denemark and Kenneth Thomas

### Research Question

The basic question addressed by the collaborative authors is: What is the most appropriate level of analysis for studying politics? The world systems approach is that the system level of analysis is the correct one from which to gain a vantage point on phenomena of interest. Brenner's position is that the nation state is the proper level of analysis, and the proper unit of analysis is class structure. Conversely, Wallerstein takes the world system as the proper level of analysis with a number of units of analysis of interest which includes classes and states. Basic to understanding this argument between Brenner and Wallerstein necessitates a cursory knowledge of Wallerstein's world system theory. Wallerstein is considered the author of what has increasingly been referred to as the world system theory he constructed as a method for understanding and classifying the nations of the world into: core, semiperiphery and periphery. As he began the exhaustive study, capitalism as the mode of production became the focus for determining that the developed world comprised the core nations; that the developing nations constituted the semiperiphery and that the nations on the periphery were those with the least capacity for controlling their position within the capitalistic system.

## Method of the Study

To begin an empirical examination of the level of analysis for studying nations within the world system, the authors concur that Brenner and Wallerstein's writings on Poland are significant. Poland was considered the ideal testing ground for determining a system level of analysis. Events in Poland were directly related to the arguments Brenner and Wallerstein make regarding the most appropriate level of analysis from which to understand political and economic events. Thus Poland was selected as a case study method for examination of the appropriate level of analysis.

Evaluative methodology by the authors determined that Wallerstein's use of a system level of analysis is better suited to explaining social and political phenomena than Brenner's state-level of analysis. Brenner's exclusive focus on events within the nation state reduces understanding of the pattern of incentives for actors within the state. The authors, however, concur that Wallerstein's position is weakened by his reliance on the process of unequal exchange in a period when the requirements necessary for that dynamic to play itself out were absent.

Brenner criticizes Wallersein's view of capitalism as ahistorical and circular because a capitalistic dynamic existed as feudalism ended and capitalism began. Brenner's position is that Wallerstein borrowed the idea of the transition from feudalism to capitalism. The circular nature of capitalism (that the accumulation of capital presupposes surplus value) is responsible for capitalistic production. Brenner criticizes Wallerstein for not examining specific class structures as an explanation for the development of capitalism rather than his (Wallerstein's) focus on the accumulation of capital.

Wallerstein contends that underdevelopment is caused by external exploitation; conversely, Brenner's position is that it results from the types of class structure occurring in the relationship of owners to labor. The underdevelopment argument continues with Wallerstein's contention that weak states in the periphery lack a strong government structure and permit underdevelopment, whereas a strong government structure will enact commercial laws for favorable trade and may exploit the weaker states. Brenner believes that this position assumes capitalist development without knowledge of whether the state is capitalist or socialist (that a weaker state results in underdevelopment is a circular proposition).

Perhaps Brenner's major criticism of Wallerstein is the issue of the method by which surplus transfer occurs. The argument surrounding surplus transfer does not seem to be complete. Brenner focuses on the increase in the price of grain as a possible explanation for a transfer of surplus to the periphery. Wallerstein, however, focuses on the balance of trade within the three tiers. The question remains: Can either the terms of trade or the balance of trade explain surplus transfer? The level of analysis for interpreting socio-political and economic phenomena is critical because it brings to the forefront the continual micro-macro debates in the social sciences.

## Evaluation

The authors synthesized the process of peripheralization by employing Poland as a case study to examine the interactive processes constituting the market place for products. "Where labor is both in short supply and too poor to serve as a market, dominant classes will have strong incentives to alter their conditions; labor will be appropriated to serve the interests of exports causing peripheralization." This analysis leads to the conclusion that while Wallerstein's emphasis on the world system level seems superior to the state-centric position of Brenner, it is not a complete system for examining social reality, because world system forces and internal political dynamics cannot stand alone.

# Second Critique

Journal: *Economic Geography* (1997) 73, 118-130
Article:  "World-Systems Theory: Toward a Heuristic and Pedagogic
          Conceptual Tool" by Debra Straussfogel

## Research Question

Can the four-capital model from ecological economics explain the
modern world system to clarify and build on the core/periphery
structure? Can this model accommodate change and transformation?
Straussfogel presents steps toward a world system that is a theory of
socio-economic transformation by reexamining the critical definition
of world system structure, the core and periphery. Then the economic
relations are redefined according to the four-capital model, and a theory
of the dynamic processes sustaining and effecting changes is proposed.

## Method of the Study

In redefining the structure in the world system, the author states that it
is a world economy, a world-polity and a world culture; that the model
must include and accommodate all the structural and transformational
logic as interdependent factors. The objective is to consider states within
the world economy as a core/periphery continuum in which roles are
exchanged according to market demands.

With the four-capital model, ecological capital, human capital, manufactured capital and institutional capital are sources of productive wealth
necessary to the functioning of the economy and its sustainability. "The
relevancy of the four-capital model to the core/periphery continuum is
in its ability to offer operational definitions along four dimensions."
For example, a country might have a high score on manufactured capital, but a low score on human capital, thus the differentiation would
indicate conditions for both core and periphery status.

The author introduces the new nonlinear science as a challenge to
the fundamental tenets of traditional science, especially the possibility
of precision and prediction. The author states that a theory of transformation of social structures is possible utilizing the general theory of
nonlinear dynamics at the micro and macro levels. Correspondence
between structural definitions and system dynamics means the transformational change at the level of the world economy can be a function

of the imposition of some major external pressure or the instabilities internal to the microdynamics of the system.

## Evaluation

The interdisciplinary focus of this article was immediately recognizable. The agency, structure debate from sociology is present in the author's attempts to redefine the structural definition for the context of a world system in which there are many levels of actors. The economic issue with respect to the four-capital model as it relates to globalization and ecology is straightforward, as is the nonlinear dynamics concept. The redefinition of the structural composition of world system theory lends credibility to the necessity for incorporating and factoring in cultural aspects into the analysis of the nation states as they are classified in either the core, semiperiphery or periphery. As the author has stated, the redefinition and the proposed model "provide the beginnings of a unifying framework defining a world of more than political states and economic zones." "It describes a world encompassing people, landscapes, cultures, social institutions, economic capacities and political tenets." Although applied theory was not a direct objective of the author, nonlinear application would have strengthened the study as well as specific examples of countries fitting into the four-capital model.

# Appendix II

## Turkish Constitution, Revised September, 1980

### Part One, Articles 6 & 7

**Article 6**. Sovereignty is vested in the nation without reservation or condition.

The right to exercise sovereignty shall not be delegated to any individual, group or class. No person or agency shall exercise any state authority which does not emanate from the Constitution.

**Article 7**. Legislative power is vested in the Turkish Grand National Assembly on behalf of the Turkish Nation. This power cannot be delegated.

### Part One, Articles 14 & 15

**Article 14**. None of the rights and freedoms embodied in the Constitution shall be exercised with the aim of violating the indivisible integrity of the State with its territory and nation, of endangering the existence of the Turkish State and Republic, of destroying fundamental rights and freedoms, of placing the government of the State under the control of an individual or a group of people, or establishing the hegemony of one social class over others, or creating discrimination on the basis of language, race, religion or sect, or of establishing by any other means a system of government based on these concepts and idea.

The sanctions to be applied against those who violate these prohibitions, and those who incite and provoke others to the same end shall be determined by law.

**Article 15**. In times of war, mobilization, martial law, or state of emergency the exercise of fundamental right and freedoms can be partially or entirely suspended, or measures may be taken to the extent required by the exigencies of the situation, which derogate the guarantees embodied in the Constitution, provided that obligations under international law are not violated.

# Part One, Article 26

**Article 26**. No language prohibited by law shall be used in the expression and dissemination of thought. Any written or printed documents, phonograph records, magnetic or video tapes, and other means of expression used in contravention of this provision shall be seized by a duly issued decision of a judge or, in cases where delay is deemed prejudicial, by the competent authority designated by law. The authority issuing the seizure order shall notify the competent judge of its decision within twenty-four hours. The judge shall decide on the matter within three days.

# Part Two, Articles 60 & 61

**Article 60**. Everyone has the right to social security.

The State shall take the necessary measures and establish the organization for the provision of social security.

**Article 61**. The State shall protect the widows and orphans of those killed in war and in the line of duty, together with the disabled and war veterans, and ensure that they enjoy a descent standard of living.

The State shall take measures to protect the disabled and secure their integration into community life.

The aged shall be protected by the State. State assistance to the aged, and other rights and benefits shall be regulated by law.

The State shall take all kinds of measures for social resettlement of children in need of protection.

To achieve these aims the State shall establish the necessary organizations or facilities, or arrange for their establishment by other bodies.

# Part Two, Articles 68 & 69

**Article 68**. Political parties are indispensable elements of the democratic political system.

The statutes and programs of political parties shall not be in conflict with the indivisible integrity of the State with its territory and nation, human rights, national sovereignty, and the principles of the democratic and secular Republic.

**Article 69**. Political parties shall not engage in activities outside the lines of their statutes and programs, and shall not contravene the restrictions set forth in Article 14 of the Constitution, those that contravene them shall be dissolved permanently.

# Part Three, Articles 75 & 76

**Article 75**. The Turkish Grand National Assembly shall be composed of one-hundred and fifty deputies elected by universal suffrage by the nation.

**Article 76**. Persons who have not completed their primary education, who have been deprived of legal capacity, who have failed to perform compulsory military service, who are banned from public service, who have been sentenced to a prison term totaling one year or more excluding involuntary offenses, or to a heavy imprisonment; those who have been convicted for dishonorable offenses such as embezzlement, corruption, bribery, theft, fraud, forgery, breach of trust, fraudulent bankruptcy, and persons convicted of smuggling, conspiracy in official bidding tender, or purchases, of offenses related to the disclosure of State secrets, of involvement in ideological and anarchistic activities, and incitement and encouragement of such activities, shall not be elected deputies, even if they have been pardoned.

Judges and prosecutors, members of the higher judicial organs, members of the teaching staff at institutions of higher education, members of the Higher Education Council, employees of public institutions and agencies who have the status of civil servants, other public employees not regarded as laborers on account of the duties they perform, and members of the Armed Forces shall not stand for election or be eligible to be a deputy unless they resign from office.

# Part Three, Article 101

**Article 101**. The President of the Republic shall be elected for a term of office of seven years by the Turkish Grand National Assembly from among its own members who are over 40 years of age and who have completed their higher education or from among Turkish citizens who fulfill these requirements and are eligible to be deputies.

The nomination of a candidate for the Presidency of the Republic from outside the Turkish Grand National Assembly shall require a written proposal by at least one-fifth of the total number of members of the Assembly.

The President of the Republic cannot be elected for a second time.

The President-elect, if a member of a party, shall sever his relations with his party and his status as a member of the Turkish Grand National Assembly shall cease.

# Part Three, Articles 109-116

**Article 109**. The Prime Minister shall be appointed by the President of the Republic from among the members of the Turkish Grand National Assembly.

The ministers shall be nominated by the Prime Minister and appointed by the President of the Republic, from among the members of the Turkish Grand National Assembly, or from among those eligible for election as deputies, and they can be dismissed, by the President of the Republic, upon the proposal of the Prime Minister when deemed necessary.

**Article 110.** The Government Program of the Council of Ministers shall be read by the Prime Minister or by one of the ministers before the Turkish Grand National Assembly within a week of the formation of the Council of Ministers, following which a vote of confidence shall be taken. Debate on the vote of confidence shall begin two full days after the reading of the program and the vote shall be taken one full day after the end of debate.

**Article 111.** If the Prime Minister deems it necessary, and after discussing the matter in the Council of Ministers he may ask for a vote of confidence in the Turkish Grand National assembly.

A request for a vote of confidence shall be rejected only by an absolute majority of the total number of members.

**Article 112.** The Prime Minister, as Chairman of the Council of Ministers, shall ensure cooperation among the minister, and supervise the implementation of the government's general policy. The members of the Council of Ministers are jointly responsible for the implementation of this policy.

**Article 113.** The formation, abolition, functions, powers and organization of the ministries shall be regulated by law.

**Article 114.** The Ministers of Justice, Internal Affairs and Communications shall resign prior to general elections to the Turkish Grand National Assembly.

The number of members to be taken from political party groups shall be determined by the President of the Turkish Grand National Assembly, and shall be communicated to the Prime Minister. Party members who do not accept the ministerial posts offered them, or who resign subsequently, shall be replaced by independent persons from within or outside of the Grand National Assembly of Turkey.

**Article 115.** The Council of Ministers may issue regulations governing the mode of implementation of laws or designating matters ordered by law, provided that they do not conflict with existing laws and are examined by the Council of State.

Regulations shall be signed by the President of the Republic and promulgated in the same manner as laws.

**Article 116**. In cases where the Council of Ministers fails to receive a vote of confidence under Article 110 or is compelled to resign by a vote of no-confidence under Articles 99 or 111, and if a new Council of Ministers cannot be formed within forty-five days of elections for the Bureau of the President of the Turkish Grand National Assembly of the newly elected Turkish Grand National Assembly, the President of the Republic may likewise, in consultation with the President of the Turkish Grand National Assembly, may call new elections.

# Part Three, Article 118

**Article 118**. The National Security Council shall be composed of the Prime Minister, the Chief of the General Staff, the Ministers of National Defense, Internal Affairs, and Foreign Affairs, the Commanders of the Army, Navy, and the Air Force, and the General Commander of the Gendarmerie, under the chairmanship of the President of the Republic.

The National Security Council shall submit to the Council of Ministers its views on taking decisions and ensuring necessary coordination with regard to the formulation, establishment, and implementation of the national security policy of the State. The Council of Ministers shall give priority consideration to the decisions of the National Security Council concerning the measures that it deems necessary for the preservation of the existence and independence of the State, the integrity and indivisibility of the country, and the peace and security of society.

The agenda of the National Security Council shall be drawn up by the President of the Republic taking into account the proposals of the Prime Minister and the Chief of the General Staff.

In the absence of the President of the Republic, the National Security Council shall meet under the chairmanship of the Prime Minister.

# Appendix III

# The Black Sea Economic Cooperation

The Black Sea Economic Cooperation is comprised of eleven states, Albania, Armenia, Azerbaijan, Bulgaria, Georgia, Greece, Moldova, Romania, Russia, Turkey and the Ukraine. On June 1992, the heads of governments from these states signed an agreement establishing the BSEC regional multilateral structure.

The International Secretariat is in Istanbul, the Black Sea Trade and Development Bank is in Thessalonika; and the BSEC coordination center for the exchange of statistical data and economic information is in Ankara. Thus the BSEC has developed a comprehensive multilateral cooperation plan covering banking and finance, exchange of statistical data, economic information, energy, transportation, telecommunications, trade, industry, agriculture, tourism, science and technology.

The telecommunications project, Dokap, a combined system of fiber optic terrestrial cable and radio link is a bus-regional project already underway. The system will connect Azerbaijan, Georgia and Turkey. In addition to the telecommunications project, a comprehensive transport network is envisaged around the Black Sea.

An important aspect of the BSEC is its flexibility. The BSEC is open to and supportive of the cooperation of other interested states through membership or as observers. This applies to countries, international organizations and companies wishing to contribute and benefit from this process. Austria, Egypt, Israel, Italy, Poland, the Slovak Republic and Tunisia have asked for and been granted observer status in the BSEC (see *The Banker,* Sept., 1993, Vol. 143, #811, 28-29).

# Appendix IV

# Turkish Work-force Participation

Thousand of person, April 1998

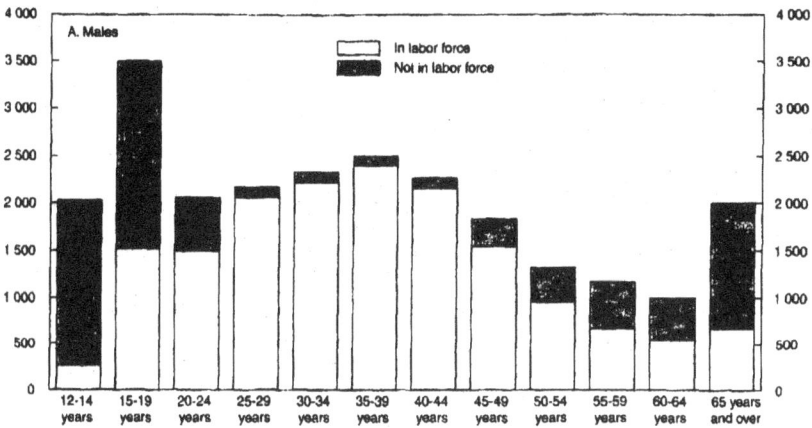

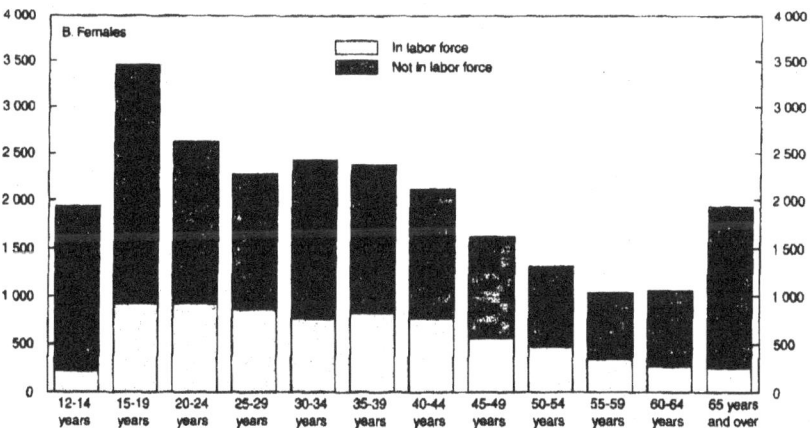

A. Males

In labor force
Not in labor force

(Age groups: 12-14 years, 15-19 years, 20-24 years, 25-29 years, 30-34 years, 35-39 years, 40-44 years, 45-49 years, 50-54 years, 55-59 years, 60-64 years, 65 years and over)

B. Females

In labor force
Not in labor force

(Age groups: 12-14 years, 15-19 years, 20-24 years, 25-29 years, 30-34 years, 35-39 years, 40-44 years, 45-49 years, 50-54 years, 55-59 years, 60-64 years, 65 years and over)

*Source*: State Institute of Statistics (1998), *Household Labor Force Survey Results*, April (OECD-1999)

# Appendix V

## Turkish Trade by Groups of Products, 1980-97

(See tables on following pages)

(a) Exports

| Commodity | 1980 | 1990 | 1991 | 1992 | 1993 | 1994 | 1995 | 1996 | 1997 |
|---|---|---|---|---|---|---|---|---|---|
| Total (US$ million) | 2,910 | 12,959 | 13,593 | 14,715 | 15,349 | 18,105 | 21,597 | 23,045 | 26,245 |
| | | | | | (per cent of total) | | | | |
| Agriculture | 64.7 | 25.5 | 28.7 | 24.2 | 24.4 | 23.5 | 21 | 21.4 | 20.8 |
| Food | 51.1 | 22.4 | 26 | 22.7 | 22.6 | 21.9 | 19.6 | 19.7 | 19.6 |
| Agricultural raw materials | 13.6 | 3 | 2.8 | 1.4 | 1.9 | 1.5 | 1.5 | 1.7 | 1.3 |
| Mining | 8.5 | 6.6 | 5.5 | 4.4 | 3.7 | 3.9 | 4.6 | 3.6 | 3.2 |
| Manufactures | 26.9 | 67.9 | 65.8 | 71.3 | 71.9 | 72.6 | 74.4 | 73.8 | 74.9 |
| Iron & Steel | 0.9 | 11.5 | 9.7 | 9.4 | 11.9 | 11.9 | 9.2 | 8.5 | 8.6 |
| Chemicals | 2.6 | 5.9 | 4.5 | 4.3 | 4 | 4.1 | 4.2 | 3.8 | 4 |
| Other semi-manufactures | 3.6 | 5.2 | 6 | 6.8 | 6 | 6.5 | 6.8 | 6.9 | 7.1 |
| Machinery and transport equipment | 2.9 | 6.6 | 7.5 | 8.8 | 8.4 | 9.4 | 11 | 12.5 | 12.7 |
| Textiles | 11.8 | 10.8 | 10.1 | 10.5 | 10 | 11.7 | 11.1 | 11.2 | 12.1 |
| Clothing | 4.5 | 26 | 26 | 28.9 | 28.7 | 25.8 | 28.9 | 26.9 | 26.2 |
| Other consumer goods | 0.6 | 1.9 | 2.1 | 2.6 | 2.9 | 3.2 | 3.2 | 3.9 | 4.1 |

Source: UNSD, Comtrade database (SITC Rev.1).

(b) Imports

| Commodity | 1980 | 1990 | 1991 | 1992 | 1993 | 1994 | 1995 | 1996 | 1997 |
|---|---|---|---|---|---|---|---|---|---|
| Total (US$ million) | 7,573 | 22,300 | 21,047 | 22,871 | 29,429 | 23,268 | 35,707 | 42,733 | 48,585 |
| | | | | | (per cent of total) | | | | |
| Agriculture | 5.1 | 12.6 | 9.9 | 10.7 | 10.5 | 10.2 | 12.6 | 11.2 | 10.1 |
| Food | 3.5 | 8.3 | 6 | 6 | 5.6 | 5 | 7 | 6.5 | 5.5 |
| Agricultural raw materials | 1.6 | 4.3 | 3.8 | 4.8 | 4.9 | 5.2 | 5.6 | 4.7 | 4.7 |
| Mining | 51.7 | 26.2 | 23.4 | 21.2 | 18.2 | 22.4 | 18.8 | 18.6 | 15.1 |
| Ores and other minerals | 2.3 | 3.1 | 3.7 | 3.2 | 3.3 | 4.2 | 3.7 | 3 | 2.8 |
| Fuels | 48.4 | 20.7 | 17.8 | 16.4 | 13.5 | 16.4 | 12.9 | 13.8 | 10.3 |
| Manufactures | 43.1 | 61.1 | 66.1 | 67.8 | 70.8 | 67 | 68.4 | 69.2 | 71.9 |
| Iron & Steel | 4.5 | 5.6 | 5.7 | 5.7 | 6.8 | 5.7 | 5.9 | 4.5 | 4.8 |
| Chemicals | 16.2 | 12.6 | 13.5 | 13.5 | 11.9 | 13.7 | 14.8 | 13.3 | 13.2 |
| Other semi-manufactures | 2.6 | 4.6 | 5.5 | 5.4 | 5.5 | 5.2 | 5.7 | 5.9 | 5.2 |
| Machinery and transport equipment | 18.1 | 31.7 | 34.2 | 35.3 | 38.2 | 33 | 32.2 | 35.6 | 38.4 |
| Other electrical machines | 3.2 | 4.3 | 5.2 | 4.8 | 4.4 | 4.7 | 3.5 | 4.2 | 4.6 |
| Automotive products | 3.2 | 6.1 | 5.5 | 6.7 | 8 | 4.7 | 5.3 | 7.2 | 9.5 |
| Other transport equipment | 0.5 | 2.3 | 2.6 | 4.2 | 6.7 | 5.2 | 5.8 | 3.3 | 3.3 |
| Textiles | 1.1 | 2.5 | 2.6 | 3.1 | 3.5 | 4.8 | 5.1 | 4.5 | 4.8 |
| Clothing | 0 | 0.1 | 0.1 | 0.1 | 0.2 | 0.2 | 0.1 | 0.4 | 0.5 |
| Other consumer goods | 0.7 | 4 | 4.6 | 4.7 | 4.7 | 4.5 | 4.5 | 5 | 5.1 |

Source: UNSD, Comtrade database (SITC Rev.1).

# Appendix VI

## Human Rights Convention Ratified by the Candidate Counties, June 1999

(see table on following page)

| Adherence to Conventions and Protocol | BG | CY | CZ | EE | HU | LV | LIT | MT | PL | RO | SK | SV | T |
|---|---|---|---|---|---|---|---|---|---|---|---|---|---|
| European Charter for Human Rights | X | X | X | X | X | X | X | X | X | X | X | X | X |
| Right of Property | X | X | X | X | X | X | X | X | X | X | X | X | X |
| Freedom Movement | O | X | X | X | X | X | X | X | X | X | X | X | O |
| Death Penalty | O | O | X | X | X | X | X | X | O | X | X | X | O |
| Ne bis in idem | O | O | X | X | X | X | X | O | O | X | X | X | O |
| Prevention of Torture | X | X | X | X | X | X | X | X | X | X | X | X | X |
| European Social Charter | O | X | O | O | X | O | O | X | X | O | X | O | X |
| Revised European Social Charter | O | O | O | O | O | O | O | O | O | X | O | X | O |
| System of Collective Complaints | O | X | O | O | O | O | O | O | O | O | O | O | O |
| National Minorities | X | X | X | X | X | O | X | X | O | X | X | X | O |
| International Convention on Civil and Political Rights | X | X | X | X | X | X | X | X | X | X | X | X | O |
| Right of Individual Communication | X | X | X | X | X | X | X | X | X | X | X | X | O |
| Abolition of Death Penalty | X | O | O | O | X | O | O | X | O | X | O | X | O |
| International Covenant on Economic, Social and Cultural Rights | X | X | X | X | X | X | X | X | X | X | X | X | O |
| Convention Against Torture | X | X | X | X | X | X | X | X | X | X | X | X | X |
| Convention on the Elimination of All Forms of Racial Discrimination | X | X | X | X | X | X | X | X | X | X | X | X | O |
| Convention on the Elimination of All Forms of Racial Discrimination Against Women | X | X | X | X | X | X | X | X | X | X | X | X | X |
| Convention on the Right of the Child | X | X | X | X | X | X | X | X | X | X | X | X | X |

X = Convention ratified   O = Convention NOT ratified

BG = Bulgaria; Y = Cyprus; CZ = Czech Republic; EE = Estonia; HU = Hungary; LV = Latvia; LIT = Lithuania; MT = Malta; PL = Poland; RO = Romania; SK = Slovakia; SV = Slovenia; T = Turkey

Source: European Commission on Human Rights

# Bibliography

## Secondary Sources

### Books in Turkish and French

Akgun, Ismail. 1967. *Turk Medeni Kanunu*. Istanbul: Matbaacilik ve Kitapcilik Muesseseleri. This work is a discussion of the Swiss Civil Code of Law.

*Değişim Belgeleri* (Documents on Change, 1979-1992). [1993]. Istanbul: Nokta. This work contains the speeches of Prime Minister Ozal, 1983-1980, and President Ozal, 1989-1993.

Erdemir, Sabahat, ed. 1961. *Milli Birlige Dogru* (Toward National Unity). Istanbul: Bakanoglu Matbaasi.

Kaynar, Resat. 1954. *Mustafa Resit Pasa ve Tanzimat*. Ankara. Akay Kitapevi. *Tanzimat* means the act of giving new order to the state. The first series of reforms dealt with the military; the second series guaranteed Muslims and non-Muslims equal rights and obligations concerning residency in Turkey.

Kubali, Huseyin Nail. 1950. *Devlet Ana Hukuku* (Constitutional Law). Istanbul. Matbassi.

Nayir, Yasar Nibi. 1963. *Atatürkculuk Nedir* (What is Ataturkism)? Istanbul: Varlik Basmevi.

Ozoguz, Nejat. 1944. *Temyiz Mahkemesi*. Ankara: Akay Kitapevi. This work describes the general characteristics of the Turkish Court of Cassation, its history, development, organization, powers responsibilities and appeal procedures.

Young, George. 1906. *Corps de Droit Ottoman*. Oxford: Clarendon Press.

## Books in English

Ahmad, Feroz. 1993. *The Making of Modern Turkey.* New York: Routledge.

Ansay, Tugrul. 1966. *American-Turkish Private International Law.* New York: Columbia University Press.

Arai, Masani. 1992. *Turkish Nationalism in The Young Turk Era.* Leiden, E. J. Brill.

Arat, Zehra, ed. 1997. *Deconstructing Images of "The Turkish Woman."* New York: St. Martin's Press.

Arrighi, Giovanni, ed. 1985. *Semiperipheral Development: The Politics of Southern Europe in the Twentieth Century.* Beverly Hills: Sage Publications, Inc.

Balta, Tahsin Bekir. 1965. *Organization and Functions of the Central Government of Turkey.* Ankara: Matbaacilik ve Ticaret.

Baysan, Tercan and Charles Blitzer. 1991. Turkey. In *Liberalizing Foreign Trade,* ed. Demetris Papageorgiou, Michael Michaely and Armeane Choksi, 1-263. Cambridge: Basil Blackwell Press.

———. 1990. Turkey's Trade Liberalization in the 1980s and Prospects for its Sustainability. In *The Political Economy of Turkey: Debt Adjustment and Sustainability,* ed. Tosun Aricanli and Dani Rodrik, 1-278. New York: St. Martins Press.

Berkes, Niyazi. 1964 *The Development of Secularism in Turkey.* Montreal: McGill University Press.

Bianchi, Robert. 1984. *Interest Groups and Political Development in Turkey.* New Jersey: Princeton University Press.

Birand, Mehmet Ali. 1987. *The General's Coup in Turkey.* New York: Pergamon Press.

Bornschier, Volker and Christopher Chase-Dunn. 1985. *Transnational Corporations and Underdevelopment.* New York: Praeger.

Brewer, Anthony. 1980. *Marxist Theories of Imperialism.* London: Routledge and Kegan.

Brinton, Jasper Y. 1968. *The Mixed Courts of Egypt.* New York: Yale University Press.

Bryant, Ralph C. 1995. *International Coordination of National Stabilization Policies.* Washington, DC: The Brookings Institution.

Brus, Wlodzimierz and K. Larki. 1989. *From Marx to the Market: Socialism in Search of an Economic System.* New York: Oxford University Press.

Carbaugh, Robert J. 1995. *International Economics*. Cincinnati: International Thomson Publishing.

Case, Karl and Ray Fair. 1996. *Principles of Macroeconomics*. Upper Saddle River, NJ: Prentice Hall, Inc.

Chase-Dunn, Christopher. 1989. *Global Formation*. Cambridge, MA: Basic Blackwell Ltd.

Chase-Dunn, C. and Thomas D. Hall. 1997. *Rise and Demise: Comparing World-Systems*. Boulder, CO: Westview Press.

DeMelo, Jaime and A. Panagariya, eds. 1995. *New Dimensions in Regional Integration*. New York: Cambridge University Press.

Emmanuel, Arghiri. 1972. *Unequal Exchange*. New York: Monthly Review Press.

Esposito, John, L. 1991. *Islam and Politics*. New York: Syracuse University Press.

———. 1995. *The Islamic Threat*. New York: Oxford University Press.

Folsom, Ralph. 1995. *European Union Law*. St. Paul, MN: West Publishing Co.

Frey, Frederick. 1956. *The Turkish Political Elite*: Boston: MIT Press.

Gereffi, Gary and Miguel Korzeniewicz. 1994. *Commodity Chains and Global Capitalism*. Westport, CT: Praeger Publishers.

Geyikdagi, Mehmet Yasar. 1984. *Political Parties in Turkey: The Role of Islam*. New York: Praeger Publishers.

Gianaris, Nicholas V. 1993. *Contemporary Economic Systems*. Westport, CT: Praeger Publishers.

Goldfrank, Walter L., ed. 1979. *The World-system of Capitalism: Past and Present,* 1-312. Beverly Hills: Sage Publications.

Gowland, D. and S. James. eds. 1991. *Economic Policy After 1992*. Brookfield, VT: Dartmouth Publishing Co.

Gunter, Michael M. 1992. *The Kurds of Iraq: Tragedy and Hope*. New York: St. Martin's Press.

———. 1994. *The Changing Kurdish Problem in Turkey: Conflict Study #270.*

Warwickshire, England: The Research Institute for the Study of Conflict and Terrorism.

Hale, William. 1994. *Turkish Politics and the Military*. London: Routledge and Kegan.

Hanioglu, Sukru. 1995. *The Young Turks in Opposition*. New York: Oxford University Press.

Heper, Ayse O. and Heinz Kramer, eds. 1993. *Turkey and the West: Changing Political Cultural Identities.* London: I. B. Tauris and Co. Ltd.

Heper, Metin. 1985. *The State Tradition in Turkey.* Beverly, North Humberside: Eothen Press.

Heper, M. and Ahmet Evin, eds. 1994. *Politics in the Third Turkish Republic.* Boulder, CO: Westview Press, Inc.

Hopkins, Terence K. and Immanuel Wallerstein. 1980. *Processes of the World-System.* Beverly Hills: Sage Publications, Inc.

———. 1982. *World-Systems Analysis: Theory and Methodology.* Beverly Hills: Sage Publications, Inc.

Huntington, Samuel P. 1991. *The Third Wave: Democratization in the Late Twentieth Century.* Norman, OK: The University of Oklahoma Press.

———. 1996. *The Clash of Civilizations and the Remaking of World Order.* New York: Simon and Schuster.

Karpat, Kemal H. 1982. *Political and Social Thought in the Contemporary Middle East.* New York: Praeger Publishers.

Katz, Mark N. 1999. *Revolutions and Revolutionary Waves.* New York: St. Martin's Press.

Keohane, Robert. 1989. *International Institutions and State Power.* Boulder, CO: Westview Press.

Keohane, Robert and Joseph S. Nye, eds. 1972. *Transnational Relations and World Politics.* Cambridge: Harvard University Press.

———. 1977. *Power and Interdependence: World Politics in Transition.* Boston: Little Brown.

Kushner, David. 1977. *The Rise of Turkish Nationalism.* Portland: Frank Cass and Co., Ltd., International Specialized Books.

Lewis, Bernard. 1968. *The Emergence of Modern Turkey.* London: Oxford University Press.

Maddison, Angus. 1995. Explaining The Economic Performance of Nations: Essay In Time and Space. In *Economists of the Twentieth Century*, 1-496. Welliston, VT: Edward Elgar.

Mango, Andrew. 1994. *Turkey: The Challenge of a New Role.* Westport, CT: Praeger Publishers.

Mardin, Serif, ed. 1994. *Cultural Transition in the Middle East.* Leiden, England: E. J. Brill Publishers.

———. 1989. *Religion and Social Change in Modern Turkey: The Case of Bediuzzaman Said Nursi.* New York: State University of Albany Press.

Martinussen, John D. 1997. *Society, State and Market: A guide to competing theories of development.* London: Zed Books Ltd.

Mehmet, Ozay. 1990. *Islamic Identity and Development: Studies of the Islamic Periphery.* New York: Routledge Press.

Nugent, Neill. 1994. *The Government and Politics of the European Union.* Durham: Duke University Press.

Onulduran, Erson. 1974. *Political Development and Political Parties in Turkey.* Ankara: Basievei Press.

Osman, Charles. 1994. *GLOBALISATION AND REGIONALISATION: The Challenge for Developing Countries.* Paris: OECD Development Center.

Ostrorog, Count Leon. 1927. *The Angora Reform.* London: London Press.

Ozburdun, E. 1981. The Politics of Clientelism: In *Political Clientelism, Patronage and Development,* ed. In S. N. Eisenstadt and R. Lemarchand, 186-197. Beverly Hills: Sage Publications.

Pinder, J. 1991. *European Community: The Building of a Union.* Oxford: Oxford University Press.

Pomfret, Richard. 1991. *International Trade: An Introduction to Theory and Policy.* Cambridge: Blackwell Press.

Rahman, Fazlur. 1982. *Islam and Modernity, Transformation of an Intellectual Tradition.* Chicago: University of Chicago Press.

Ramsaur, Jr. Ernest E. 1957. *The Young Turks.* Princeton: Princeton University Press.

Rustow, Dankwart A. 1987. *Turkey: America's Forgotten Ally.* New York: Council on Foreign Relations Inc.

Saribay, Ali Yasar. 1991. The Democratic Party, 1946-1960 in *Political Parties and Democracy in Turkey.* Martin Heper and J. Landau, eds. New York: Routledge.

Swann, Dennis. 1996. *European Economic Integration.* Brookfield, VT. Edward Elgar.

Tapper, Richard, ed. 1994. *Islam in Modern Turkey: Religion, Politics and Literature in a Secular State.* New York: St. Martin's Press.

Taskin, Fatma and Erin Yeldan. 1996. Export Expansion, Capital Accumulation and Distribution in Turkish Manufacturing, 1980-92. In *The Economy of Turkey Since Liberalization, ed.* S. Togan and V. Balasubramanyam, 137-155. London: Macmillan Press Ltd.

Togan, Subidey. 1994. *Foreign Trade Regime and Trade Liberalization in Turkey During the 1980s.* Brookfield, VT: Avebury Ashgate Publishing Ltd.

Tekeli, Sirin. 1995. *Women in Modern Turkish Society, A Reader.* London: Zed Books Ltd.

Thomas, Vinod, Ajay Chhibber, Mansoor Dailami and J. DeMelo, eds. 1991. *Restructuring Economies in Distress: Policy Reform and the World Bank.* New York: Oxford University Press.

Toprak, Binnaz. 1981. *Islam and Political Development in Turkey.* Leiden, England: E. J. Brill Press.

Viotti, Paul R. and Mark V. Kauppi. 1993. *International Relations Theory: Realism, Pluralism, Globalism,* 2nd ed. Needham Heights, MA: Allyn and Bacon.

Wallace, William. 1994. *Regional Integration: The West European Experience.* Washington, DC: The Brookings Institution.

Wallerstein, Immanuel. 1995. *After Liberalism.* New York: The New Press.

———. 1983. *Historical Capitalism.* London: Verso Press.

———. 1980. *The Modern World System,* Vols. I & II. New York: Academic Press.

Wildavsky, Aaron and John Clark. 1990. *The Moral Collapse of Communism.* San Francisco: Institute for Contemporary Studies Press.

## Technical Sources

### *Books*

Horn, Robert V. 1993. *Statistical Indicators for the Economic and Social Sciences.* Cambridge, MA: Cambridge University Press.

Organization for Economic Co-operation and Development Economic Surveys: *Turkey.* Paris: OECD Development Center.

OECD. [1980-1981].

OECD. [1981-1982].

OECD. [1982-1983].

OECD. [1983-1984].

OECD. [1984-1985].

OECD. [1985-1986].

OECD. [1987-1988].

OECD. [1989-1990].

OECD. [1990-1991].

OECD. [1991-1992].

OECD. [1992-1993].

OECD. [1993-1994].

OECD. [1994-1995].
OECD. [1995-1996].
OECD. [1996-1997].
OECD Economic Surveys: Turkey, Reforming Social Security. [1998-1999]. Paris: OECD Development Center.
Social Science Citation Index. [1976-1980]. Vol. 18. Philadelphia: Public Institute for Scientific Information.
Social Science Citation Index. [1985]. Vol. 5.
Social Science Citation Index. [1990]. Vol. 5.
Social Science Citation Index. [1999]. Vols. 1 and 2a.
World Bank. [1996]. *From Plan to Market: World Development Report.* New York: Oxford University Press.
World Bank. [1997]. *The State in a Changing World: World Development Report.* New York: Oxford University Press.
World Bank. [1988a]. Turkey Country Economic Memorandum: Towards Sustainable Growth. *Report 7378-TU.* Washington DC.

## *Journal Articles*

Ahmad, Feroz. 1988. Islamic Reassertion in Turkey. *Third World Quarterly* 10 (2): 750-769.
Ayata, Sencer. 1996. Patronage, Party, and State: The Politicization of Islam in Turkey. *Middle East Journal* 50 (4) (Winter): 40-56.
Brown, Phillip M. 1923, 1924, 1927. The Treaty of Lausanne and The Lausanne Conference. *American Journal of International Law* 17, 18, 21 (April, January, July): 114-293.
Chase-Dunn, Christopher. 1975. The Effects of International Economic Dependence on Development and Inequality: a cross-national study. *American Sociological Review* 40 (December): 720-38.
Denemark, Robert and Kenneth Thomas. 1988. The Brenner-Wallerstein Debate. *International Studies Quarterly* 32: 47-65.
Kadioglu, Ayse. 1996. The Paradox of Turkish Nationalism and the Construction of Official Identity. *Middle East Studies* 32 (2) April: 177-192.
Keohane, Robert and Joseph Nye. 2000. Globalization: What's New? What's Not? *Foreign Policy.* Spring: 104-119.
Krugman, Paul and Anthony J. Venables. 1996. Integration, Specialization and Adjustment. *European Economic Review* 40 (2) April: 73-85.

Kubali, H. N. 1957. Modernization and Secularization as Determining Factors in the Reception of Foreign Law in Turkey. *International Social Science Bulletin* 9: 56-68.

Lijphart, Arend. 1971. Comparative Politics and the Comparative Method. *The American Political Science Review* 65: 682-93.

Lipstein, K. and others. 1957. Reception of Foreign Law in Turkey. *International Social Science Bulletin.* 9: 59-68.

Nadolski-Glidewell, Dora. 1977. Ottoman Secular and Civil Law. *International Journal of Middle East Studies* 8: 517-543.

Proff, Heike and V. Harald. 1996. Effects of World Market Oriented Regional Integration on Developing Countries. *Intereconomics* (March/April): 34-56.

Reich, Robert. 1990. Who Is Us? *Harvard Business Review.* (January/February): 53-64.

Sakallioglu, Umit Cizre. 1996. Liberalism, Democracy and the Turkish Center-Right: The Identity Crisis of the True Path Party. *Middle East Studies* 32 (2): 142-161.

Straussfogel, Debra. 1997. World-systems Theory: Toward a Heuristic and Pedagogic Conceptual Tool. *Economic Geography* 73: 118-130.

Thayer, Lucius. 1923. Capitulations of the Ottoman Empire. *American Journal of International Law* 18 (October): 219-230.

Velidedeoglu, H. V. 1957. The Reception of the Swiss Civil Code in Turkey. *International Social Science Bulletin* 9: 41-63.

## *Institutional Article*

Hartler, Christina and Sam Laird. 1999. The EU Model and Turkey. *World Trade Organization Staff Proceedings,* 4-18. Geneve: Trade Policy Division.

## *Newspaper Articles*

*Helsinki Watch.* 1992. Vol. 4, no. 9, p. 14.

*Istanbul Milliyet.* 1992. 27 March, p. 42..

*New York Times.* 1996. 12 July, p. A8.

*Istanbul Turkish Daily News.* 1995. 9 October; p. A3.

*Wall Street Journal.* 1999. 16, 19 April; pp. A7, A.11; 16, 27, August; pp. A10, A6; 26, November; p. A1; 13, December; p. A25.

*Wall Street Journal.* 2000. 16, 25, February; pp. A23, A17.

# Index

# About the Author

Dora Nadolski began work on the Ph.D. in Political Science at Georgetown University, and completed the degree at the University of Missouri. She has taught at Rockhurst University, Park University, the University of Missouri at Kansas City, Robert College in Istanbul and Northwest Nazarene University. Awards include a Fulbright, a National Endowment for the Humanties in Islamic statecraft, a Social Science Research Council Fellowship in Erfurt, Germany, and from 2005 to 2008, selected for outstanding achievements, and for biographical inclusion in: *Who's Who in America*, *Who's Who in American Women*, and *Who's Who in American Education*. Interest in Turkey began with Peace Corps service as an instructor at the Adapazari Lisesi, and at the Middle East Technical Institute in Ankara.

www.ingramcontent.com/pod-product-compliance
Lightning Source LLC
Chambersburg PA
CBHW020355270326
41926CB00007B/442